Rescue Your Child's Education Now

Foster Lifelong Learning Through Homeschooling

M. J. CLAUS

Blessings

M J Claus

WESTBOW
PRESS®
A DIVISION OF THOMAS NELSON
& ZONDERVAN

WestBow Press books may be ordered through booksellers or by contacting:

WestBow Press
A Division of Thomas Nelson & Zondervan
1663 Liberty Drive
Bloomington, IN 47403
www.westbowpress.com
844-714-3454

Scripture quotations taken from The Holy Bible, New International Version® NIV®
Copyright © 1973 1978 1984 2011 by Biblica, Inc. TM
Used by permission. All rights reserved worldwide.

Interior Image Credit: EJC Photography ejcphotography@fastmail.com

ISBN: 978-1-6642-7515-7 (sc)
ISBN: 978-1-6642-7517-1 (hc)
ISBN: 978-1-6642-7516-4 (e)

Library of Congress Control Number: 2022914975

Print information available on the last page.

WestBow Press rev. date: 08/15/2022

Endorsements

"Very informative, and she discussed every point of view. I like the fact of the explanation of structured education vs. unstructured learning. Everyone is different and it's OK. Do what works for your family and lifestyle. I'm a firm believer that if you put Christ in your children's lives, they will learn to be kind, generous, helpful, and compassionate. I love how M. J. Claus explains the importance of children learning what works for them."

—Zaharoula (Zazi) Leggett, former special education paraprofessional and parent

"If you find yourself visiting or revisiting the questions of "Should we homeschool?" and "Could we really homeschool successfully?" this book is for you! M. J. Claus walks with you as a friend, helping you to *Rescue Your Child's Education Now* with practical, easy-to-follow guidance and advice with which to begin and sustain your homeschooling journey."

—M. Mansfield, EdM, Boston University, homeschool educator and parent

"I heard Norman Geisler say in a lecture many years ago, "Sending your children to public schools would be like the Israelites sending their children to the Canaanites for seven hours a day." I became an advocate for private Christian schooling and homeschooling immediately. M. J. Claus will get you started on the right foot for your homeschooling journey. It is more imperative today than ever before."

—Dr. Joseph Cardamone, pastor of First Baptist Church, Wolfeboro, New Hampshire

"M. J. Claus's book is a gem if you are looking for the courage to break out of public schools. She is there with all her successes and failures to cheer you on in every way!"

—Kay Page, former public school teacher and international teacher trainer for Youth with a Mission's College of Education, University of the Nations, currently a prison volunteer in Maine

"M. J. Claus does a delightful job encouraging readers that they can indeed homeschool. She provides foundational steps to getting started and ideas for thinking outside the box for your children's education."

—Patricia Hetticher, author

This book is dedicated to my children: the two I gave birth to and all their homeschooled friends who are like sons and daughters to me. May you love the Lord your God with all your heart, mind, soul, and strength and love your neighbor as yourself. I hope that you too will one day homeschool your children and teach them to respect the Lord, to love truth, and to be independent lifelong learners.

Contents

Contents

Foreword

M. J. Claus has been my dear friend for many years. Like I did with my seven children, she has homeschooled her two through all their school years. I can testify that she excelled in raising two kind and thoughtful children into exemplary adults who care deeply about the world around them and who actively involve themselves in caring for other people.

M. J. herself is a very creative person, often thinking outside the box for solutions to difficult problems. She recognized early on in raising her children their creative natures, and she created space around them to allow them to grow into their potential as thinking, caring human beings, just as God designed them to be. No parent would want less for their own children.

This intentional, nurturing tending to the strong growth of her children can be, perhaps, understood by M. J.'s own growth. Very early in her life, she demonstrated an enthusiasm for life, especially with plants. Her discovery of plants and her desire to learn to identify them in fields and forests drove her to learn as much as she could about them. She delights in searching out growing plants that are difficult to find in the natural settings. She is now a certified expert in the identification and care of plants. She leads children and adults on forays into forests so that she can share her enthusiasm for plants, especially in their natural habitats. She brought this enthusiasm into her homeschool and found that her interests and skills adapted very well to teaching school topics and life lessons to her children. Having the courage and determination to remain fully herself as she built her homeschool gives M. J. Claus the proven right to encourage other parents to *go for it* as they consider homeschooling their own children.

Her expert knowledge of what plants need to be strong and healthy is reflected in the environment she created for her children to grow in wisdom and understanding. She knows that plants need all the right elements to grow well: sunlight, water, soil with good nutrients, and space to grow freely into the beauty of the mature plant that God had designed it to be. Children need the same.

This book is full of M. J. Claus's powerful, creative ideas for homeschooling children. Her ideas were forged in her own home and have proven to be wonderfully effective. May this book be a springboard for many families' adventures into homeschooling.

Sara Lapointe, homeschool teacher and parent

Acknowledgments

Thank you to the following:

- my parents, who taught me to love the Lord and seek Him first
- my husband, who has supported and encouraged me to write our story and been my faithful partner in life for more than thirty-four years
- my children, who endured having me as both mother and teacher
- EJC Photography for the beautiful close-up images of my dish gardens
- the homeschooling community, friends, and family, who have shared their lives and adventures with me; I cannot name you all here so I will thank you in person
- the ladies in my writing group, Line-It-Up Writers, Kay, Sara, and Patti, who listened to my story as it was written, edited every draft, and encouraged me to tell my unique experiences
- homeschool graduate and content writer Catherine, who reorganized and edited the manuscript
- the WestBow Press team who helped me put this book into print

Much love to you all!

Introduction

EJC photography

The Homeschool Adventure

When it comes to your child's education, you should be a consumer, so seek to provide the best education you can for your child. Don't settle for just a good-enough education. The outcome is going to affect your family, your community, the world, and them for the rest of their lives. You should know your reasons for homeschooling. When it gets tough, having your goals written down will help you remember why you began. Over time, your goals may change, but you will need to have an initial direction to launch.

Homeschooling is an adventure, but it is not the best choice for everyone. If you are thinking about homeschooling, or have already begun, this book introduces seven principles to aid you on this journey. It will help you know how to begin homeschooling, guide you through choosing resources and keeping records, teach you how to find your parenting style, and discover how your child learns best. Later, common myths about homeschooling will be presented and addressed. Lastly, you will learn how to cultivate a *lifestyle of learning* so that your children become self-motivated to seek resources of all types and embrace learning throughout their lifetime.

Consider the cost if you choose *not* to homeschool. What are your children absorbing from the public school culture that may conflict with the values of your family and undermine your family heritage? Is your public school curriculum revising history? What societal pressures will they face too early before they have had time to develop a sense of who they are and what they believe? Political agendas sweep through the education system, weaving their way into the textbooks and into our children's minds. Through schools and under the pretense of health and safety, partnering organizations seek to break down modesty and promote promiscuity among children, encouraging them to experiment with their bodies before they have a sense of how their bodies are developing. Pressures weigh heavily on children to look like models, to perform like athletes, to experiment with drugs, and to explore sexual deviancy.

In government-funded education, Common Core standards profess to know what is best for every child and mandate what each child must do to meet those milestones and when they are ready to move forward. Standardized testing supposedly guides the child toward a future profession. This testing and Common Core standard cannot replace the loving, caring, nurturing knowledge of parents who understand their child and where their passions and God-given talents lie. Parents who spend a lot of time with their children can better discern when and how their children are ready to learn. If you have noticed this not-so-subtle social agenda that has made its way into your child's education, take charge of it now and reverse the effects.

When considering the cost to homeschool your child, first consider the *investment* you will make in their future. Then you can count financial costs. Investments take resources you already have. You must put forth something of value with the expectation and hope of a good return on that initial capital that you put out. You want to make sure you are investing wisely and have trustworthy information about the investment and a way to measure how that investment is doing. With homeschooling, just as with parenting, you don't always see a quick return on your investment. It takes time to develop momentum, to organize resources, to develop a plan, to execute it, and to measure progress.

Usually, one parent gives up a career to manage their child's education. Sometimes the cost of materials, classes, and transportation is high, but it doesn't have to be. One of our most memorable homeschooling years was when we had no extra money to spend. After my husband had cancer treatments, we were all home and able to spend precious family time together. Even though we didn't have the resources or energy to go on trips, to buy textbooks, or to pay for music lessons or dance classes, we enjoyed the outdoors and spending the time together teaching our children what we know.

If you have always wanted to homeschool or have explored other options after trying public and private school, think about what support you already have. Are you committed to home educate your child? Do you have a family that will help you? Perhaps it is overwhelming to think about homeschooling all your kids full time. You could start by working with one or two children at a time, helping them learn to read and increasing their math skills or another area you feel confident in. There are many ways to find a homeschool community. If your area doesn't have a good support system, consider creating a homeschool group or co-op. You may even consider a career change or perhaps work remotely in a different state or region if it puts you closer to the support you need. Some families relocate to another area for greater home education freedom and better local support.

Friendships

Sometimes within the homeschooling community, it can be challenging to meet new friends or to keep up with old friendships. One way we were able to help our kids meet people was to be invitational. When a new family moved to the area and started homeschooling, I invited them over to share our books and materials and introduce them to some of the activities in our area. We always offered to drive ours and others' kids to events, to pick up and drop off friends, and to give rides to any others who were joining a field trip or sport. In that way, we got to know their friends and families. Before our kids were in high school, we moved to the next town, a little farther away from our son's friends but right in the same neighborhood as our daughters' two best friends. This was a great opportunity to carpool to regular weekly activities, such as youth group, chess club, soccer games, and other special activities, such as plays, dinners, and proms. My husband and I got to know these families well and became good friends. Another way to meet new people was to accept invitations.

Going to homeschool beach day, soccer games, Fourth of July festivities, and joining ski club provided a great way to meet other homeschoolers.

We have always felt that if we foster a loving, fun environment for our kids and their friends (and feed them), they will want to hang out at our house. We don't have a large home or a huge yard. We have lived in a rented small house for several years and squish everyone in, heating up frozen pizza and playing cards, but for six years, we have hosted a Saturday night group for teens and young adults. It started out as a small game night for our kids and their friends. As time went on, our son and several of his friends graduated from high school and went off to college, but they returned on Saturday nights when they could. Our home is the place where they can come every week and not have any expectations put on them. They have found acceptance here and rest from pressures at work, school, or home. One year seven of our sixteen "kids," including our daughter, were graduating from high school or college, and they all wanted us to host a party. We have also hosted an engagement party for one of our "daughters," several birthday parties, and going-away parties over the years. Even when our son was away at his last semester of college, several young adults still came over for pizza and games every weekend. These are the "sons and daughters" I dedicate this book to.

Not Always Easy

I highlight the positive aspects about homeschooling to encourage you to evaluate your current educational plan for your kids and give it a try. To be honest, just like anything we pursue that has immense value, it isn't always easy. There are many obstacles to overcome and challenges you will face. From financial problems, family illnesses, and trauma to other circumstances beyond your control, we all navigate what life throws at us in diverse ways. While you may decide to homeschool for one year or twenty, the time you spend together as a family will be a treasured memory.

Unless your circumstances throw you into the new adventure of homeschooling overnight, explore your options surrounding education. Interview family and friends to find out who is going to support you through this journey. Explore the opportunities for education in the area you live or where you want to live. As a consumer, know your options. Get what you want for your children's education. Don't just settle for the local public school. There is a sacrifice to homeschool, but consider the sacrifices you make to *not* homeschool. Weigh the benefits by talking to homeschool graduates and parents who have homeschooled their children. Consider the cost both financially and morally to you, your kids, and their futures as you decide what is the best way to educate your child now.

CHAPTER 1

Our Story

EJC photography

Before Kids

I met my husband when I was a junior in high school and he was a senior. We dated for four years, through the rest of high school and college. I earned an associate degree in landscape horticulture. We were married in the late summer of 1992, when he had one more semester of college to finish, graduating with a bachelor's degree in engineering.

I started delivering flowers and caring for interior plants for a florist after we were married and moved in together. Little did I know that my landscape horticulture degree, and the training I received as an interior plant care technician, would lead to a twenty-eight plus year career as a small business owner.

I am the youngest child of six. But I'm very much like an only child because my closest sibling is over eight years older than I am. And my eldest brother is almost fifteen years older than me. We had good, loving, caring parents, who were married almost sixty years before my dad went to be with the Lord.

Mom lived for another eight years without him. We surrounded my parents with love and care through their last days. My family didn't have a lot of money when I was growing up. But we had an abundance of love and laughter together. I attended public school because it was the default, we didn't even consider private school, and homeschooling was unheard of at that time.

My husband is the middle child of three. His younger sister sustained a head injury when she was seven, he was twelve, and their older brother was fifteen. That changed the family forever. Friends started to gather in prayer around them and supported them through the tragedy. Although now she has difficulty walking and speaking, Francine is a tremendous blessing and joy to others.

She has remained at home, with the dedication and devotion of her loving parents to care for her. Although Francine attended a special school for people with medical challenges, until high school, she was able to attend the same public high school as my husband and I were, with an aide. Like me, he also attended only public schools.

Although we were married nine years before we had our first child, homeschooling was always the plan for the early years of *our* children's education. During those years, together without children, we knew several families who homeschooled. We admired how the grade school children communicated with people of all ages, not just their peers. In addition, we saw how they could entertain themselves and were not in constant need of attention. The middle school children we knew interacted graciously with adults and could carry on conversations on a variety of topics.

And in the high school youth group that we led, we saw the homeschooled children run activities and welcome newcomers with ease. I still laugh when I hear people say homeschoolers don't get socialized. That is not at all what we witnessed or experienced.

The families worked together to serve the community and supported one another. We were impressed that the kids were independent thinkers, not following the pop culture, attitudes, styles, or voice of the day like we had experienced in school. As a result, we decided to homeschool long before our son and daughter were born.

With Kids

Our goals in educating our children were to develop character; give our kids a solid, God-centric education; and expose them to the world we lived in, only when it was appropriate for them to know. This included opportunities for them to explore their interests. And it kept them out of popular, secular culture and indoctrination of progressive, antifamily, anti-American propaganda.

All through the process, our aim was to cultivate a love of learning in our children. And to help them develop the skills they needed to study what God called them to do, with the talents He gave them. To develop character, we didn't shield them from the challenges we faced in our own lives, whether it was health or financial difficulties or arguments we had.

We encouraged them to face the day before them with joy, determination, and bravery. When they resisted doing hard work, my husband would say, "It builds character." We chose study materials that supported our Christian heritage and a creationist point of view. We gave them a solid, focused education.

When the kids were older and able to discuss the different worldviews of religion and science, we introduced other viewpoints. They were then able to listen, interpret, discuss, and compare their personal views with others and make their own decisions.

When we felt they were ready, and when opportunities arose to expose them to the world we lived in, we revealed the good, the bad, and the ugly parts of humanity. We did our best to walk them through it. You must go *through* tough times, not under or over them, to get to the other side. Some of the things our children had to face were earth-shattering, and it took us back to our Heavenly Father, for shelter.

One consistent, heartfelt attitude that I could not have gotten through homeschooling without was humility. I often turned to God in prayer, not just when I was out of answers and couldn't think of how to handle a situation but daily for direction and wisdom. From the time our little boy was in first grade, I was involved with Moms in Prayer, an international ministry for women, who gathered weekly to pray for our children and a local school. Together with faithful Christian women, we prayed for each other's children throughout our homeschooling years.

And you can still work, aid elderly parents, attend college, and volunteer in the community while homeschooling. Just as children fit into your life, education can fit into your life too. We had many seasons in our homeschooling life. I ran my own interior plant care business and always worked, at least one day a week, outside the home, in addition to homeschooling full time.

Since childhood, I have had a love for plants. In college, I added to my passion for plant identification as I earned an associate degree in landscape horticulture. I started my own interior plant design and maintenance care business when I was only twenty-three. At that time, I also completed training to become a master gardener. Twenty-eight years later, I am still self-employed and continue to be the "plant" manager for the same company, supplying care for over three hundred interior plants each week.

As the kids grew up from infants to teenagers, they were invited to join me while I watered and cared for the plants. But most of the time, I found a friend or relative for them to spend the day with. Joining other families' homeschool lessons gave them social time and experiences with other homeschool families.

While with Grammy and Papaw, they spent precious hours getting to know family history and cooking. They learned how to make jam from the berries Papaw grew and his delicious apple slices dessert from his own apple crop. Grammy taught them how to be thrifty shoppers and to get all the deals. And of course, as many grandparents do, she paid for everything when they shopped together.

My husband has worked from home and long hours outside the home at different periods through the years. After graduating with a degree in mechanical engineering and working in the field of manufacturing for several years, he decided to pursue a career in architectural design. He went back to school in the evenings, when our son was a baby, to earn a degree in architectural engineering. Both jobs have posed challenges and provided benefits to homeschooling.

Being the youngest of six children and born late in the lives of my mom and dad, I have been sandwiched between having young children and aging parents. My children had the privilege of knowing my parents, who were sixty-seven and seventy-six, when our son was born. As my parents aged and needed more help, we were able to spend many days with them.

Homeschooling gave us the flexibility to do this. The relationships built a strong family bond. My parents, Nannie and Poppa, gave our children a perspective from real life experiences that we just don't see today. They went through it when it happened. Poppa told stories of his training during WWII, when the war ended, and how they celebrated afterward.

Nannie was the youngest of twelve children and grew up in New York City, just after the Great Depression. As a family, we pulled together to assist my parents with rides, grocery shopping, and personal care as they aged. I can't even begin to explain all the precious lessons our children learned through that experience. But here is a report written by our son when he was nine years old after he interviewed my dad—

Charles enlisted at age seventeen. He graduated from Brooklyn Technical Institute in January of 1944. He signed up to join the army and was called in May of 1944. He was in training for two years in Yuma, Arizona. The war ended and Charles (Poppa) was locked on base. He could hear the local Indians cheering. At that time in Yuma, the Indians lived in mud huts near the base. It was not a city at that time. Charles had his basic training in Biloxi, Mississippi, and Sioux Falls, South Dakota. He was in radio school to train as a radio mechanic/waist gunner. At that time, a sergeant in the army made only $78 a month. Charles was able to decode Morse code messages in under five minutes. During training one day, he decoded messages quickly and was in a tent working when a plane in training burst into flames and hit a nearby tent where his buddies were resting. The plane, tents, and his comrades were burned in the accident. Another day at training, he was put out in a small cabin to release skeet for practice shooting. When his time came to release and no skeet appeared, his officer came to the cabin and found him locked in with a rattlesnake. He shot it. After the war, Charles was in Panama City, Florida, and Inglefield, Florida. He had a class A pass and worked only one out of every six days.

Now in her late teens, our daughter has been visiting her father's parents in Upper Michigan every fall and helping them out. After Papaw's treatments for leukemia, she stayed for two months and helped him plant trees and work in the yard. She learned about deer hunting and landscaping from her Papaw. Working at the local Republican headquarters with her, Grammy gave her experience election campaigning. Together they volunteered weekly to hand out flyers and discuss the election with people in the community. These experiences coincided with the way she learns and made a huge impression on her life. As a young adult, she decided to move in with her grandparents.

Although neither Craig nor I was introduced to homeschooling when we were children, we made the decision that we would commit to this style of education for our own family. At first, we observed how other families homeschooled, and then we embarked on the adventure with their advice and support. We developed our own style. After many years of collaborating in a supportive community, we naturally became a resource for other parents who had decided to homeschool their children. Together with other families, we raised our children and provided them with an excellent education.

CHAPTER 2

Understanding Your Parenting Style

EJC photography

Your Parenting Style

The way you parent your children will greatly impact the way you homeschool. Spending many hours a day together may cause you to reevaluate how you parent. Your style may change as the dynamics of your family change with time and with size as well. Regardless, understanding your parenting style is a key step in discovering your homeschooling style. You may not realize how connected they are. It helps to understand yourself and other homeschooling families you will be working with if you recognize unique styles and respect the way they each operate. Perhaps you'll find you tend to gravitate toward parents whose style is like yours. Be aware though of the many styles, and be open to collaborating with people to share ideas and remembering your common goal of homeschooling your children.

We started to notice how different families managed their child's education when we began collaborating with other parents to organize homeschool field trips, sports events, and classes. Putting a very structured-style parent in charge of organizing monthly field trips to historic places, for example, resulted in well-planned trips with a lot of families attending and repeated adventures. When an unstructured-style parent planned a social event, such as an open invitation to a park or to a state beach where there was no need for reservations or advance tickets, we had a lot of fun, and the children had more of an opportunity to direct the activities. Both styles have benefits.

Structured-style parents may set up concrete boundaries, goals, and the means of obtaining them. You may have already chosen what the consequences of not meeting those goals will be. Children will know clearly what is expected of them. Structured-style parents may want to buy a boxed curriculum with all the supplies included: textbooks, teacher guides, schedules, supplemental reading materials, science kits, and even tests to go along with it.

Unstructured, free-style parenting may have the opposite approach, allowing children to decide what they want to study and how and when they want to conduct a task. As a result, day-to-day goals change with the interests of the child. Free-style parents may find this method works well for them. It doesn't mean children are uneducated; it means their time is unstructured. Unstructured parenting is permissive, allowing the child to choose what they most like to study and giving them the freedom to choose how.

Most people fall somewhere between a structured, authoritative style of parenting and an unstructured, free style of parenting. However, since you as the parent oversee your children's education, give them some sort of framework in which to learn. Guide them to the subjects they need for success. We found a great title for our homeschooling style: *eclectic*. We used a wide variety of curricula, styles, and resources depending on what was available to us and what circumstances we were dealing with at the time. Repeatedly, we revisited our goals to see if we were following them.

Focused Learning

One guide we used through all the years of homeschooling was to allow at least half an hour per grade level per day for focused learning. That meant that in kindergarten our daughter would sit with me and practice writing short words for half an hour one day, work with numbers for half an hour another day, and play with magnetic alphabet letters to practice spelling a third day. At the same time, our firstborn was in second grade. We were spending an hour and a half a day together learning various subjects, such as spelling, addition, and reading. The rest of the day, each child would study independently by learning through interactive play. Creating characters and vehicles with building blocks, playing store with a toy cash register, going to the park, and writing a story with friends were some of their favorite pastimes. Not as fun, but sometimes necessary, was helping with household chores, including cleaning out our bearded dragon lizard habitat.

As our children grew, instruction shifted from me as primary teacher to group classes offered in the community, independent study online, and from a DVD course. Starting in middle school, both children began taking classes online through a charter school, meeting weekly with their teacher via computer. By the time the kids were in high school, they had become more independent, and study time increased to five to six hours a day. This aligned with our parenting style. We directed our children to start to take charge of their own schedule and manage their responsibilities. Subjects could be "chunked," which means studied two at a time until finished. As they dove into a topic, the students immersed themself in study to master it. Once those were finished, they moved on to another two subjects. This is how our daughter managed her high school courses and graduated early.

As parents, we worked hard to train our kids to one day become autonomous adults able to take care of themselves and others—like us when we get older! Those values are woven through the fabric of our homeschool life. From teaching them how to wash their own laundry, plan and cook meals, and drive a car to serving others, sticking close to a friend going through tough times, and taking care of someone when they are ill, we guide them through life. God is with us through all these circumstances, leading, guiding, and comforting us. You and I are not alone on this journey.

Our eclectic style created a flexible frame. Allowing the kids to use different methods or take their time to learn the subject was how we allowed flexibility in our schooling plans. Expecting the kids to study certain subjects and to show progress was the frame. We accomplished this by gathering materials and studying on our own, exploring museums, using textbooks, and attending group classes. At home, we used many diverse sources from which to learn, often obtaining pre-owned or borrowed materials. That way, if they weren't a good fit for our kids, we hadn't made a huge financial investment in them. Through this approach, we were able to explore many different curricula, educational games, books, as well as other educational resources. Once we understood what each child's learning style was, we developed or bought materials and supplies to support those learning styles.

Worldview

Our parenting style influenced the way we taught our kids by the curricula we chose and how we chose to use it. We sought to build character and a moral compass into our children with a love for God and for other people. Through this lens, we chose educational resources and materials that either supported that goal or made a good basis for discussion about it. We did not avoid controversial topics or shelter them from the world, popular books, or movies. When viewing disturbing movie scenes, we discussed them together as a family. When popular movies were released based on books, we first read or listened to the book and then watched the movies together. When we met people with differing opinions, styles, or religious beliefs, we talked with our kids about it. This opened discussion about society, politics, religion, and other sensitive topics that created a base foundation view for them to explore on their own as they matured and established their own worldview.

> Do not conform to the pattern of this world, but be transformed by the renewing of your mind. Then you will be able to test and approve what God's will is— his good, pleasing and perfect will. (Romans 12:2 New International Version)

Sometimes I still wonder, *Did our children develop skills they need to study what God calls them to do?* That is not always clear, and there are times when our young adults don't know what the next plan is for their lives, but still, I know God has a perfect and pleasing will and a specific purpose and plan for their lives. It is never too late to learn, so if they don't have all the skills they need, they can learn as they go. That's exactly what we have taught them to do!

Mom, I won't learn everything I need to know right now.
I'll learn what I need to learn when I need to know it.
(C. Claus)

When I question my success as a parent, at first, I want to weigh it against the world's standards of success, such as independence, financial prosperity, and popularity, but that's not good enough. Do they honor God and show virtue? When I sit down and have a conversation with our son, or I listen to our daughter's opinions on friendship, I think, *Yes, they each honor and respect the God of our Christian faith, and yes, they understand virtue and respond to situations in a way that honors God.* I see this in the way they relate to their friends, when they make choices of whom to spend time with, in the activities they will take part in, and in what they reject. I see it in the way they relate to people in the community, at camp, or at the library. The director at the camp our son worked at for seven summers once greeted me when I picked him up from camp, shook my hand, and said, "He emanates Christ in everything he does, and he smiles at the face of adversity." Both of our offspring have their own faith different from my husband's and mine. It isn't that they are little robots following everything we do. On the contrary, they are quite different in how they live out their Christian faith.

When I evaluate our parenting success regarding our Christian faith, I know that we did the best we could in humility, with prayer, and with purposeful consideration of our Christian worldview. Now we are launching our young adults into the world with support and guidance. We did not eject them into society where they must face the difficulties and pressures of adult life on their own. Parenting, guiding, directing, and being there to help your kids adjust to adult life is another step beyond homeschooling. Parenting doesn't end when your youngest child is eighteen or has graduated from high school.

CHAPTER 3

Discovering How Your Child Learns

EJC photography

Learning Styles

When I started homeschooling, I didn't understand that there are different learning styles. I knew that I learned best by watching someone do something, having them explain it to me, and then trying it myself. I knew that I struggled to learn the way I was expected to in the public schools I attended. Most of the time I had to read from a textbook and then answer questions based on the reading. I wasn't allowed to write in the book. I wasn't allowed to read the test questions out loud to myself, doodle, or take notes during the tests. Everyone in my school was taught as if there were only one style of learning and one way to teach. My husband and I wanted our children to have a better learning experience than we had.

By the time I was in college, I had figured out that I could learn what I needed to know for a test by listening closely to the lecture, writing down what the teacher wrote on the black board, and then memorizing the material by reading it several times the night before. I could ace the test by knowing just what the professor was looking for and getting it out of my head before I forgot. What I learned in college came by way of the labs. The hands-on experience of pruning trees and shrubs on campus and learning to identify them by their leaves, stems, and flowers helped me remember them. I'll never forget the time I pruned a very large juniper bush right next to the main building of the college. I was having a wonderful time snipping here and there, using the loppers to get one last branch off, and then oops! A huge branch fell off, leaving a large, awkward gap in the luscious, green growth of the juniper and exposing the concrete wall of the building that was in dire need of paint. The whole class was watching, and the professor said with a smile, "Now we just learned that you need to be careful which branch you prune." To this day, I check twice before lopping off any large branch!

I am a tactile and visual learner, so as I began homeschooling young children, teaching them through hands-on experiences was easy. However, as they started to develop their own styles of learning, the challenges began. I could not figure out why our son had to have an audiobook on all the time. Reasoning that it is good for him to listen to classic stories, then stories about history, then stories about geography, science, Greek mythology, etc., I kept obtaining audiobooks to feed his curious ears. *But how—just how does he remember all this while he's building LEGO brick creations for hours at the same time?* I wondered. I made him stop, read a book or two, and do some writing and math in a workbook, but like a stretched rubber band, his mind snapped right back into the building zone. We used to yell, "Pizza!" just to get his attention. That is when I began to research learning styles.

Our son is an auditory learner. We were extremely fortunate to have a vast number of good-quality, educational, easy-to-access audiobooks and audio files available to us. The stories he chose were mostly historical fiction with engaging characters. The person reading the story in the recording was just as important as the story itself and had to be engaging and use his voice to keep the listener's interest. Once I let the textbooks go and allowed him the time to build with blocks and listen, our son's knowledge expanded beyond the region we lived, beyond the history of the United States, beyond the earth, and even beyond the earth's atmosphere as he explored stories of black holes and nebulae. He sailed the great seas with pirates, explored the deep oceans with whales, and fought battles with chivalrous mice.

Our son told stories about what he learned as he listened. As an auditory learner, he accumulated a large vocabulary at an early age and could articulate what he wanted to communicate. I do not have many physical papers or workbooks to show what he studied, but what he learned then is showing through in his artwork and in his conversations now that he's an adult. Believe me: it was hard to measure his progress in school because it was often presented verbally. One way I recorded what he learned was to have him dictate information to me or to a computer.

Another way was to record it in audio format or a video. I held on to any writing he did and printed anything he typed.

Our daughter has a different learning style—kinesthetic and visual. She loves to capture images in digital format to help her remember people, places, and events. In middle school, she enjoyed reading books while also listening to an audio recording of the same story so she could hear the pronunciation of the words while she read. Once she sees a printed word and hears the proper pronunciation, she remembers the spelling forever. It's like she has an imprint of that spelling in her mind. She also enjoys hands-on artwork and drawing to remember an event, person, or place.

On one occasion, she learned to draw cartoon-style stick figures from a local cartoon artist. The professional offered a free six-week class at the local library for students after school. For her world history timeline, our daughter combined pieces of plastic, fabric, wood, and other natural materials to dress up the pen or pencil stick figures she drew. We have albums filled with creatively drawn stick figures wielding tiny plastic swords, wearing fabric capes, and wearing feather in their caps. Her creativity is evident in this precious keepsake!

After I observed how she learns best, I modified lessons to include field trips and projects that involved experiments. Everyday tasks that needed to be accomplished anyway turned into learning opportunities. Shopping was a math lesson, cooking was a science lesson, and making bread was kitchen chemistry. When our daughter was a senior in high school, she ran her own business selling clothing online. Learning math had been a struggle for her until she had a practical application for it. That was how she found that her mathematical strength was in business math. Being a hands-on learner, workbooks and textbooks didn't satisfy her educational needs. She needed that hands-on experience to comprehend and to remember what she learned.

I have many boxes of artwork and stories she wrote incorporating events in history and characters she developed. We kept all the portfolios and the world history timeline she made. My favorite story written by her showed how she understood the relationships among historical figures. We saw that our daughter was interested in the communication between the people and not just the mere facts of dates, places, and people. Through her writing, and the dialogue of the characters, she was able to express what she had learned about history.

Creating Space

If you know your child's learning style, prepare a personal space that fits that style. When you eventually figure out their needs for a prime learning space, it will become their favorite spot to go. I have tried to teach an auditory learner with textbooks, a visual learner with audiobooks, etc. It was a constant struggle. Once I set up a space where our son could put together building block creations and listen to audiobooks without interruption, we were all in a better mood! Once I understood the different learning styles, it didn't take long to figure out how he learned best. I know that you cannot always accommodate your child's prime learning atmosphere.

Learn to get along, and to do the best you can with what you know and what resources you have. (M. J. Claus)

Look around your home for a place to store specific educational materials. Bookshelves, entertainment center shelves, kitchen cabinets, and storage boxes in the closet are all places we have used when we did not have a designated school room. We cleared off the dining table after breakfast each morning and used that as our group study area. We could spread out cards, books, or papers to work on for the day. If we were not finished by dinnertime, we would stack the papers and put them aside for the next day. We had a "bonus" room off the kitchen that was sort of a hallway but was wide enough for bookshelves and a play space when the kids were little.

Additionally, each child had a to-go bag holding two or three lessons to take along when we had to run errands or travel to visit family.

When the kids were six and eight, we set up a play store and library for our daughter where we went daily to order play food and check out books. Our son had an area rug to spread out his building block creations and had storage bins in his closet for putting his toys. Your older children may want to be in their bedroom or even fix up a part of a shed or tree fort to do their schoolwork in. How many kids get to study in a tree fort? For five years, we had a travel trailer. When it was parked in the yard, it made a great creative play space. Friends and neighbors came over to the "café" for a cold lemonade and ice cream sandwich or could choose another treat from the menus the kids made. It was a great space for tea parties too. These are just a few examples of how to use the space you have now.

Find creative ways of making room that fits your child's learning style. Being a visual learner, I enjoyed having posters, wall maps, and books related to the subject we were studying. Our daughter enjoyed this too and added to the decor with her artwork. She and I loved visiting museums repeatedly and playing with the interactive displays. On the other hand, our son did not care for my elaborate decorations or care to visit the same museum for a second time. He said he learned enough from one visit.

Setting up a learning environment is important and will save you time and energy overall. I am not talking about a classroom. A learning space may be a corner of the bedroom, under a table in the playroom, or a space under the stairs. This is a space for one child to do his or her independent study in his or her own style. An auditory learner may enjoy movies, plays, or an audiobook subscription. If this describes your child, consider investing in a personal listening device, headphones, or earbuds and give him a quiet place to listen to stories and music away from pets or siblings. Make time to read aloud together as a family. This is a wonderful way to connect with your auditory learner, to discuss the topics he listens to, and to find out what he is learning from the reading.

What Is Important

When you get down to the root of teaching, what is important is that the child learns and then can communicate to you or others what he or she knows. You then record it to prove that they have learned something. There are many online tests you can take to find out what your learning style is. Think about it, test yourself, and practice using that style to see if you agree. Ask your child how they like to learn something new to gain insight into their learning style. It may be different from yours, and then you have some studying to do to find out how to best accommodate them so they can learn most successfully. This may be different from what you expect. I was flabbergasted that our son could learn just by listening to audiobooks.

You get to be the one to assess your child's outcome, to record what they learned, and then to continue presenting material to them until you both find an effective way for them to meet the goals you have set. This is indeed a great responsibility, but it is also a great privilege. As their parent, you know them best. You do not need a degree in education to teach your child or to understand how your child learns.

CHAPTER 4

Planning and Preparing

EJC photography

Now that you have decided to homeschool, there are so many things to do. Remember you are a role model for your kids. They will follow your example one day even if they appear to be resisting it now. There are five simple steps to take as you begin homeschooling. From understanding the home education laws where you live to selecting resources and materials, take it one step at a time and enjoy the process. As you set goals, a budget, and a financial plan for investing in your child's education now, you are embarking on a journey. While assessing your child's academic abilities may take time, it is well worth the effort to know at what level to continue their studies so they are learning at a grade that is best for them.

Home Education Laws

Find out the laws for homeschooling in your state; the procedure of notification that you are homeschooling may begin at once. You may have to notify your school district by sending a letter of intent to the resident school district or school your child was attending within a few days of your decision to homeschool. Where we were homeschooling, parents had five days after commencement of a homeschool program to notify the school district. In other states, you may not have to notify anyone. Know the laws yourself, and do not just follow what the local school tells you is needed. School officials are remarkably busy and do not always know or understand the home education laws or the updates as things change. Do what you need to follow the law, and then do what is right for you and your child. Don't be afraid to contact your state representatives or the department of education. Call the home education advisory council if you have questions. Let them know your needs and desires for the education of your child.

We would not have the freedoms we have today without the bravery and boldness of homeschooling pioneers, such as the Lapointe family, who helped to pave the way for us to homeschool our children today. They spoke up and exercised their rights to educate their children themselves when there were no rules or guidelines for homeschooling.

Here is part of their story:

In 1983, I was lent a book on homeschooling. I had never heard that families were doing this. I spoke with my husband and said that I would like to try this, at least for a year. He agreed. At the time, the oldest of our three children was five years old, and his sister would be four in the fall of 1984, our first year of homeschooling. We were the first family to homeschool in the town we lived in and even made the front-page headlines of the local paper. And so, I started teaching first grade and kindergarten. I found a curriculum provider, which I used for a few years, and then selected my own favorite publishers for our school materials. The hard part for us was having to go before the local school board each summer to explain once again why we thought the public school was not good enough for our kids. By the state's homeschool laws, we were required to have the approval of the local school board each year to homeschool. I was so thankful when the state homeschool laws were modified to benefit the homeschool community, and we no longer had to do this. At the school board meetings, my husband was very diplomatic and reassured the school board members that we were simply seeking the *best* opportunity for our children and that we were instructed by our God to raise our children in the way they should go. This meant for us that we should spend quality and quantity of time with our children. We taught at home for twenty years for, eventually, our seven children. It was hard work, but oh so rewarding! The outcome has been that six of our seven graduated from college, and all are well-adjusted adults, gainfully employed, with five married and now fourteen grandchildren among them. One of our daughters was selected to attend the US Naval Academy and is now a lieutenant colonel in the US Marine Corps. Parents can do so much more than they are aware of for their children. There is no redoing those important years for laying a solid foundation in our children's lives. (Sara Lapointe, homeschooling mom of seven)

Homeschooling, Not Just Remote Learning

There is a difference between *homeschooling* and *remote learning*. Many children, especially recently, are remote learning, doing their studies from home through an online program or during government school closures. Students who are remote learning for the whole school year, or for a period, are not by law homeschooled because they are legally attending another school. Homeschooled students get most of their educational direction from a parent. While the laws vary from state to state, homeschooled students answer directly to their parent or guardian who follows state laws. I am not a legal advisor. You need to find out the current home education laws in your state and follow them.

Homeschool laws may include notification to a participating agency, such as the local school district or a private school, of

- commencement of the homeschool program
- a list of materials and resources
- a scope and sequence of your educational goals
- attendance, including hours spent on each subject
- annual reporting at the end of the school year
- annual portfolio evaluation from a certified teacher

- annual testing from a certified testing service
- attendance in a group program

When someone says they are homeschooling their child because the school is temporarily closed, it is not necessarily true. Their child is learning remotely, having video conferences with their teacher or entire class over the internet. The parent is not in charge of choosing what material the student is learning. They have not had to do research to find out what their child needs to learn, choose and purchase materials, give assignments, and oversee schoolwork. A parent of a child doing remote learning in this case does not have to test for knowledge or do a myriad of other responsibilities a homeschooling parent has to do; therefore, they should not say they are homeschooling.

Academic Assessments

Assess where your child is academically. Start with a reading assessment test. Any child with reading difficulties should get primary attention to work through this as early as possible. Reading difficulties, learning disabilities, and other challenges are harder to correct as children get older. Seek help for these early if you do not feel like you have the knowledge to address them yourself. There are easy assessments to use to determine how many phonics sounds, letters, or numbers your child understands. Do not pressure a child to read or to write in the preliminary stages of homeschooling. Just let him explore and see what he already knows before you develop an education plan. I cannot stress enough the need for early intervention in this area. Make it a priority to assist your child with learning to read. Developing writing skills can come later. Not all children can learn both simultaneously.

These are the commands, decrees and laws the Lord your
God directed me to teach you to observe in the land that
you are crossing the Jordan to possess, so that you, your

children and their children after them may fear the Lord your God as long as you live by keeping all his decrees and commands that I give you, and so that you may enjoy long life. Hear, Israel, and be careful to obey so that it may go well with you and that you may increase greatly in a land flowing with milk and honey, just as the Lord, the God of your ancestors, promised you.

Hear, O Israel: The Lord our God, the Lord is one. Love the Lord your God with all your heart and with all your soul and with all your strength. These commandments that I give you today are to be on your hearts. Impress them on your children. Talk about them when you sit at home and when you walk along the road, when you lie down and when you get up. Tie them as symbols on your hands and bind them on your foreheads. Write them on the doorframes of your houses and on your gates.

When the Lord your God brings you into the land he swore to your fathers, to Abraham, Isaac and Jacob, to give you—a land with large, flourishing cities you did not build, houses filled with all kinds of good things you did not provide, wells you did not dig, and vineyards and olive groves you did not plant—then when you eat and are satisfied, be careful that you do not forget the Lord, who brought you out of Egypt, out of the land of slavery. (Deuteronomy 6:1–12 New International Version)

For middle school students, give reading, writing, and math assessments. Test how many correct words your student can read per minute. Assign a few writing assignments to see samples of her writing. If you ask for samples of poetry, short story writing, a descriptive essay, and a book report, you can understand what she knows and where she still needs to develop reading and writing skills. Then using a variety of evaluating methods, such as oral presentations, written assignments, quizzes, and even art, you can find out how much she knows about the subjects you have chosen for her before buying materials. If you are taking your child or children out of another school, talk to the school and get all records and teacher evaluations before you purchase homeschool materials. In addition, you may choose to hire a teacher to evaluate where your child is academically to know at what level to continue teaching those subjects.

In training up children in God's ways, we need to pay heed to Deuteronomy 6. It speaks of parents making the decisions, not the government. In this training, perhaps the single most important subject is reading. Even math is just another language to the reader. Our enemy would love to totally take reading out of the children's curriculum. If a child can read, they can read the Bible. In understanding this, the one training must understand that government schools in general are failing. If children are not taught well, statistics show that nonreaders often end up in prison. Search online for the prison/school pipeline. (Kay Page, former public school teacher and international teacher trainer for Youth with a Mission's College of Education, University of the Nations, currently a prison volunteer in Maine)

You may choose to administer standardized tests, both for evaluation and so that your child is familiar with testing. There may be times when testing is necessary to move on to another field of study, to earn a certificate, to apply to college, or to get a job. Even so, standardized testing is not a good assessment of knowledge for every student. For a few years, we chose standardized testing instead of a portfolio evaluation. The results did not reflect much of what each child had learned but satisfied the requirements of the law in our state at that time.

Do not worry about assigning a grade level at first. It does not really matter what grade a child is labeled as because you are just starting. Your student can be at a fourth-grade math level, sixth-grade science level, and tenth-grade spelling level. Remember the goal is to make progress and to prove that he or she has made progress. If she skips necessary information because someone thinks she should be at a higher grade level, she may have difficulty understanding it later. Do not let the grade level label hinder your goals. Allow flexibility. Most homeschoolers I know exceeded expectations with regard to success, depth of knowledge, and speed of learning. If homeschoolers start off behind a grade, they often end up skipping a few along the way, especially in subjects that they are enthusiastic about.

I cheered when one mom told me her sons taught themselves several subjects in their high school years that she did not even know they had studied. Both her sons passed College Level Examination Program (CLEP) tests in these self-taught subjects. These tests are administered by the College Board and enable students to earn college credits if they achieve satisfactory scores in certain subject-specific tests. This is the same company that administers the Scholastic Achievement Test (SAT) that many colleges require for admission. She was pleasantly surprised to find that her sons earned college credits from following their passions.

In our case, our firstborn took an exceptionally long time to learn to read, but once he began, he caught up to "grade level" very quickly and became enthusiastic about reading adventure stories. One of the reasons we decided to homeschool was also so that our children could learn at their own pace, getting help and extra instruction in areas they needed it and being able to learn at an accelerated pace when they could. That is one of the benefits of homeschooling.

Patricia Hetticher, author and homeschool mom of three, shares from her experience.

> If you have a child who develops slowly in reading, try to incorporate different ways of learning for his other subjects. One of my children learned most things early on through hands-on science experiments, instructional videos, and the mechanics of taking things apart and putting them back together again. Kitchen appliances that no longer work, inexpensive thrift store treasures, and free finds will give your child ample hours of learning. Our child eventually caught up with his peers with reading and even reads for enjoyment as an adult.

> Forcing a child to read textbooks and complete worksheets and tests for every subject matter before they have the necessary reading skills to do so will turn them off to learning and crush their God-given curiosity for exploring and understanding their world.

Goal Setting

Write down your homeschooling goals, post them on the refrigerator, and tell them to your friends and family who ask why you are homeschooling. As you consider your goals, think about who your students are. Who is going to manage the homeschooling, give instruction, and evaluate success? How many children and what ages are they when you begin? When we started, our plan was to homeschool through third grade because I thought that was all I was qualified to teach. I thought I had to be educated in child psychology and child development or be a teacher to homeschool past third grade. However, once we met other families who had homeschooled their older children and we ourselves were having a lot of fun learning with our kids, we wanted to continue. I found that everything I presented to my children came through the lens of my passion for science, plants, and woodland animals specifically. This kept *me* interested in teaching.

You can draft a scope and sequence, which is a plan for what you will teach and how you plan to go about it. Some states require this. *Scope* means ultimate intention, and *sequence* means order and succession. For kindergarten, you may include in your math scope that you will teach reading and writing numbers one through ten and practice counting when you put away groceries or set the dinner table. The sequence would indicate that you are going to teach the numbers in order from one to ten. I wrote a scope and sequence, even though I never had any formal training to do so. It was just natural for me to write out what our goals were and how we planned to accomplish them. Also, for each subject, I gathered materials and put them on the dining table with hope that the kids would be as excited as I was to begin our next adventure together. We lived in a flexible frame, willing to adjust to the changing needs of our family as life brought us new opportunities and challenges, but the frame or scope and sequence helped me get started and stay on track for our long-term goals throughout the year.

Financial Planning

Look at finances, and set a budget. This does not have to be large. We had a fantastic homeschool year even when we did not have any extra money to spend. Several local libraries offered free membership, and we visited often, taking part in their activities, borrowing books, and using their museum passes to get into local museums. Our town library offered $20 back if we brought in a receipt from any museum we attended, up to three times per family. I bought a membership at a children's museum that had a reciprocal pass with other area museums, giving us discounts and free admission to programs and tours at a wilderness center, planetarium, history museum, and others. Along the East Coast, the Highland Foundation offered Free Fun Fridays, giving free admission to a different museum every month. We spent precious time together as a family and enjoyed the company of our friends when they joined us at a museum for only the cost of travel. I am a bargain hunter and found many ways to stretch a dollar.

One family I met decided to homeschool their daughter with special needs because she was not making progress in the private or public school systems. When studying WWII, they took her to Germany because she was a kinesthetic learner and enjoyed learning through experiences. Whatever your budget allows, keep in mind the goals that you set for your kids.

Gather a list of resources available in your area. A kinesthetic or a visual learner who seems to need to touch everything may learn well by visiting museums, parks, and local businesses and by going on field trips. An active child may use a playground, fields, or an area to ride his bike to burn off some energy after studying spelling words. Are there homeschool groups or play days offered in your area? Is there a youth center or youth group nearby? What sports can your children take part in with the recreation department or a local school? There are probably many more opportunities to take advantage of in the area you live than you are aware of.

As you get started, take this opportunity to build godly character into your kids' lives and help them become responsible team players in this broken, fear-filled world so they will shine God's light on an otherwise dark universe. (M. J. Claus)

Remember to cherish the time together as a family as you plan what and how to study and as you prepare to embark on homeschooling. You are investing in the future. Everything you do now will affect the kids for a lifetime. Together you are shaping, guiding, and supporting your children to learn, not just to gain knowledge but also to be wise and discerning.

CHAPTER 5

Choosing Educational Resources

EJC photography

One of the most daunting tasks for new homeschool families is choosing educational materials. It is indeed a huge decision. When you understand the needs of your students, you can better fit a curriculum to their learning style. Before you buy anything, check to see what resources you already have. There are nontraditional assets all around you, such as historical places in your town, parks and museums in your city, and family members and neighbors with specific talents, experiences, and hobbies who are willing to share their knowledge. Begin with what you have, and add to the collection as you need more.

Your choices for resources and materials are practically endless. Below I explain a few options.

Resources

Public Schools

In some states, the law allows home educated students to participate in public school activities and classes. Homeschoolers may be allowed to take part in afterschool activities and sports, band, chorus, physical education, or other programs. One of our neighbors sent her daughters to the public middle school to supplement their home education. One child participated in a writing class, and another took a gym class. Check with your local school to find out the law and how and when to enroll in public school programs. You will have to follow the laws in your state as not all states allow homeschoolers to participate even though they pay school taxes.

Charter Schools

Offering focused learning, such as arts, sciences, or classical and Socratic learning, a public charter school receives some government funding. Public charter schools are government funded but independently operated so they can offer curricula different from most public schools. Parents do not have to pay out of pocket for their child to attend a charter school, but they do for a private school. The charter school may charge a small fee for homeschoolers to participate in some of their courses or programs. Where we live, there is a popular liberal arts online charter school that offers middle and high school courses online to state-resident students for free. Many homeschoolers take at least a few courses through this program. Our son earned an associate degree in liberal arts through this school.

Private Schools

Many private schools offer access to homeschoolers. However, there may be a charge for participation. There also may be prerequisites, testing, and different ways of record keeping involved with participating in classes or activities at a private school. A private school does not necessarily receive government funding. It is funded independently, and students pay tuition to attend.

Online Courses

Classes are offered online through organizations from all over the world; some are even free. High school students can take classes online for college credit. Younger students can take a course or two from an online school. Check the laws in your state to see how many courses your child is allowed to take at another school and keep their status as homeschooled. While I was homeschooling, in our area, students could take up to four classes at a time at a private, charter, or public school in person or online. If he or she wanted to take five or more classes at once from another institution, they would no longer be considered homeschool students.

Cooperatives or "Co-ops"

In a co-op, families arrange to meet regularly and offer classes for their children. Teachers can be volunteers or paid professionals, but most often parents collaborate to teach classes together for the families involved in the cooperative. Our co-op offered courses once a week for elementary students and joint classes for middle and high school students. One of our groups met at a local campground retreat center. They allowed us to use the cafeteria, classrooms, playground, beach, basketball court, baseball field, and other amenities one day a week. It was a small, campus-type atmosphere in which we enjoyed eating in a cafeteria, taking recess at the playground, and going swimming after school. We commissioned a music teacher to meet individually with students throughout the day. Parents whose children had private lessons paid him independently. Other classes included history, literature, and science taught by the parents who brought their children to the co-op. Every parent was expected to teach at least one class. This was a terrific way for our students to take lab sciences and discuss great works of literature with others. Another group we were part of met at a church and used the classrooms, sanctuary, meeting room, and playground. We met one morning a week and then had lunch together afterward.

Group Classes

Group classes can be offered for a one-time class or for several weeks or months. These differ from cooperatives in that they are offered by one teacher with several students while co-ops are a collaborative effort by several adults and children. We have offered or taken part in group classes in churches, historical buildings, libraries, a private home, a community center, school, and even outdoors at a park. Often a parent teaches a group class, but it is also fun to invite someone from the community to come and tell students about their job. We have had a corrections officer teach a six-week self-defense class, an artist teach a high school art course, and even an older homeschool student teach sewing to younger students. There are many people out there willing to share their talents.

Museum Programs, Community Classes, and Library Programs

Like group classes, many museums offer workshops and courses online or in person. Where we live, homeschool students are welcomed into the museums to explore, to learn, and sometimes to help with the presentations. Many museums offer special homeschool group discounts for the programs. There are also community classes offered locally. While these are generally run for adults, if you ask, they may admit a student or two. Libraries offer programs and are happy to admit homeschoolers. Our kids took cartoon drawing, painting, and other lessons from professionals in the field for free through our local library. Libraries that take government funding must supply public programs like these as a public service. They also often have museum passes for their patrons to check out, giving free or reduced admission. We used all these services to reduce the expense of field trips.

Job-Shadow

This involves going to work with someone for a day or two to see what they do. Homeschoolers can take a day to job-shadow a parent, neighbor, or someone who works in a trade they are interested in. This allows them a tiny window into that field of work. It gives them a chance to ask questions about the position and what skills and training are needed to get the job. If they like it, they can learn more, and if they don't, they can try something else.

Volunteer

Include volunteer work as a resource for education. It is good to add this to a resume or high school transcript. People who give of their time and resources to help others are generous, selfless people. Spending time with these folks supplies another way for children to see caring, kind, giving ideals in action. Through volunteering, one can learn how to take care of one's own responsibilities while also giving to the needs of others. Opportunities abound in every area of society, from clearing trails for snowmobiles to sitting and playing cards with older folks or picking up trash on the roadsides. You can even consider volunteering as a family.

Our kids volunteered on a regular basis with a few different organizations. When our daughter was in middle school, she volunteered at a garden center for a month. Joe, who plowed our driveway in the winter, owned the garden center. He let our fourteen-year-old daughter volunteer there to learn how to care for the plants and to meet and greet customers; she also learned about watering, weeding, and keeping the flowers looking great. The librarians at our local library knew her from the time she was born, so when she was fifteen and we went in to ask if she could volunteer there, they were happy to give her the opportunity. Soon, they invited her to apply for a job as a librarian's assistant. This was a terrific opportunity for her to meet, help, and interact with more people from town. She learned much about the history of our town and the people who grew up there by hearing stories from the patrons who visited the library almost daily. Besides history, she learned marketable skills, earned money, and earned high school credit for English and library science.

Our son started volunteering at a local summer camp when he was fifteen. He started as a general helper for the staff, and over the many years he volunteered and worked there, he was on staff as a counselor and director of the boys unit. Working at camp gave him opportunities to learn responsibility for himself and for others. He spent two months away from home every summer. In this way, he learned how to interact with many different people and to work on a team to make camp the best experience possible for each camper who attended. In addition to being a meaningful way to give back to the community, volunteering can also lead to further work opportunities.

Employment

When your child is old enough, he or she can get a part-time job. Following local employment laws in your state, a student can start working a job part time after school or help run a family business. This is a terrific way to learn a variety of skills. In some states, the local school superintendent or a parent can fill out "working papers" for their child to be employed between the ages of fifteen and seventeen. Younger children can start informal chores for neighbors and friends of the family by babysitting, walking dogs, or shoveling snow. Check employment laws in your state.

Internships

An internship is usually an unpaid position (although it may be paid) in which the purpose is to learn a skill or trade. There is usually a written plan of what is expected of the intern and what the business will instruct. This is a wonderful way for a student to see what a job is like and what skills are needed for the position without a long-term commitment. As a homeschooler, the student is learning while working so she can earn credits even if she is paid. On a transcript, do not count this as both work experience and course credit. It is one or the other. As the guidance counselor of your homeschool, you can coordinate with the business offering the internship to write the educational plan if they do not have one. Tailor it to what your child wants to learn from the experience, check progress, and record changes in the plan. We outlined a course in library science when our daughter interned at the local library.

Recreation

Living in a rural community, we have many opportunities to be outdoors. The town's recreation department offers sailing, swimming, golf, tennis lessons, and more. There are also hiking groups, mushroom walks, letterboxing, and in the winter, skiing, ice skating, snowmobile riding, and sledding. You can count these as extracurricular activities, part of a physical education course, or even as a science or history lessons in some cases. Take advantage of the free offers by the recreation department, or start your own group. Go geocaching or letterboxing to get outdoors and see the local attractions in your area. Go to an amusement park and study the history of the park, the marketing scheme, popularity by season, and the physics of the rides. Have students consider the sanitation and food sources for the concession stands. These are all ways to make a field trip more educational. Follow the interest of your students, however, so you don't bore them with work and ruin the experience for them.

Movies

Include movies among the resources you use. There is a movie out there for every topic your child will study. We have the technology to access movies now like never before in history. Look for movie lists to go along with the subjects you and your child choose to study. Some might be a little graphic for younger children when subjects such as war are studied, so preview the movie and watch some with your child to explain to them the challenging scenes. We let our children watch popular movies about a young wizard named Harry a few years after the movies came out. First, they had to read or listen to the book; then we watched the movie together so we could discuss the topics and how the spiritual message in the story compared to our own beliefs. We did that with many literature series of movies that were based off popular works of literature.

TV Series

If your family sits and watches television together or if your kids and their friends watch a series, use it as a catalyst for discussion. Whether the characters are like your social group or not, you can discuss how they interact with one another. Discuss relationships, healthy and unhealthy, and recognize heroes or heroines in the story. Our family designated at least one night a week to watching a TV series together while cuddling with our cats and eating popcorn. We intentionally did not have cable TV or satellite, so we streamed all the movies or shows or rented VHS tapes or DVDs. Sometimes in a few weeks we binge-watched a series we really enjoyed in the frigid winter nights of New England. Some of the shows we watched led to in-depth discussions about topics, such as friendship, family dynamics, and school choice. We bonded, laughed, or cried together when one of the scenes brought up memories of people we missed or traumatic experiences we'd been through. I always included a list of the shows we watched together in the kids' portfolios with the movie and book lists.

Educational Materials

Teaching materials go beyond the book, chalkboard, and computer. Any physical object can be a catalyst for learning. Starting with young children in the kitchen, all the tools, furniture, and even food are materials for doing math and science and learning your family's history. Take, for instance, an old recipe box from your grandmother. You and your young child pull out a recipe for her famous cinnamon rolls, shop for the ingredients together, gather all the supplies, prepare the scrumptious goodies, and share them with your neighbor. Throughout the process, you talk about the dough rising and baking. You explain how the cinnamon is harvested, how the sugar tastes on your tongue, and how the icing melts on top and then hardens as it cools. That's science. Then you reminisce about baking them with your grandmother in her home many years ago, the apron she wore, the curtains she had hanging in her kitchen window, etc. That's family history. When you bring them to your neighbor to share the tasty, freshly baked cinnamon rolls, that's generosity.

Textbooks

You can use textbooks. Older versions of textbooks are much less expensive and still have vast amounts of information. While newer versions may have updated history or scientific data, older editions also contain valuable information sometimes not included in newer texts. Read parts of the text to figure out how it lines up with your family homeschool philosophy before using it. In some cases, the text might have a great layout or be well-written but also have ideas contrary to your homeschool philosophy. Just be aware of this and work with your child to understand the ideals portrayed in the text and how they are different from what you believe and why.

My father often helped me with my high school government and history homework so that he could tell me about his firsthand experiences in WWII and how they related to what I was studying. He was forty-five years old when I was born. He had many experiences to share. I listened to his firsthand experience, and he explained why his views were different from what were in the textbook. When he told me why he thought the way he did, I understood it much better and remembered those lessons. Even then, I could see how the views expressed in the textbooks were different from how my dad and my mom, as well as my aunts and uncles, had experienced life. Together, we looked at what material I was expected to learn for school and discussed how it was similar or different from what he experienced. You can do this for your children when you carefully choose the material they study.

Whichever textbook you choose, you'll find that some will have quizzes and tests included in them while others will have supplemental test books you can buy to complement them. One benefit of textbooks is that they can be easily transported around. The student can do his or her work anywhere with no excuse for not getting their work done while waiting for a sibling at ski club, fencing, or dance. Lessons can be scheduled, and the student can perform tasks independently, including using the answer key to check answers. However, while some students work well independently in textbooks, others do not. If you find your student struggling with following directions in the book or unable to complete the assignments, you may want to do a learning style assessment again or find a different text.

I also recommend supplementing any textbook with biographies, autobiographies, and interviews with people who have experience with the topics in the book. Granted, this may take a year or two to get through a textbook, but time isn't the issue when it comes to a good, solid understanding of a subject. If the child is interested and wants to explore a topic more, let him.

DVDs

Many publishers offer DVD courses. These can be presented as a lecture or instructional video. Homeschool high school students often get their science labs this way if there are no local group classes offered. Two people can form a group and watch the DVD together and then perform the experiments. Look at your local library for DVD courses. Purchase them or sign up online for a membership to get instruction and teaching of the topics you want. My son learns most of what he is interested in by searching for the topic online and including the word *tutorial* in the search bar. This way, he gets a link to an instructional video.

Workbooks

Workbooks are also portable and supply an effortless way to measure progress. Once a student can read, he or she can follow the directions in the workbook. They are produced for any subject and any grade level. At one time, I thought this was the way to learn most subjects. Some workbooks are indeed well formatted to encourage critical thinking and to test the knowledge of the material presented; however, many are not. Be careful when choosing a workbook to make sure it isn't just set up to teach a child to read and spit out information like a copy machine.

Art Supplies

As simple as crayons and paper, art supplies do not have to be extensive or expensive. Provide your children with at least a few colorful supplies to express his artistic side. Sometimes my kids couldn't find the words to express a wooded, overgrown, old railroad bed in the fall, but they were able to draw it on an Artist Trading Card. I put it in the portfolio. There were times when they enjoyed drawing cartoon characters. They wanted to illustrate their history lessons simply with paper and a pencil. Being extremely sensitive to feel and touch, our son would not use a pencil, so he had a set of erasable pens. All throughout our daughter's studies of ancient history, she created a scrapbook. She drew prominent characters, places, and events on small cards and glued them into a multipage album. She used this throughout her school years to look back and help her remember the lessons. The supplies were simply paper, pencils, markers, and sometimes a feather or scrap of fabric.

Deciding what educational materials to use is important. Remember though that it is also important how you use them. Make the curriculum work for you. After buying or creating your own learning plan, evaluate and assess what you are using. See how it is working for each child. There are times when you just need to forge on and complete what you started, and other times when you may just throw it out the window and start all over with something new. That is one of the benefits and freedoms of homeschooling. Even if it doesn't work for you, perhaps another child will benefit from that same curriculum. You can save it for another child in the family, sell it, or donate it. I bought used books for high school and sold them for the amount I paid for them after we were finished with them. Putting together resources for learning a subject was one of my favorite parts of homeschooling. I hope you enjoy it too.

CHAPTER 6

Keeping Records

EJC photography

There are many good reasons for keeping a record of your child's education. From the preliminary stages when a child writes or draws their first letter on paper, to later years when they write a lengthy high school book report, parents often keep at least some documentation of their child's progress. First, it is much easier to see progress when you have older work to compare it to. Celebrate milestones, such as finishing a reading program, a first prize won at a contest, or when your child makes your family's favorite recipe alone. Second, the law is different in every state, but your state may require you to keep a record of the work your child completed each year. In our state, we had to keep a homeschool portfolio of the last two years for each child. This portfolio included a sample of each subject studied in the beginning, middle, and end of the school year. For example, in your portfolio you could include tests from math, lab reports from science, and a few samples of writing for English. However, not all portfolios have to be samples of work on paper. Get creative and include photos of projects your child worked on, artwork she created, or a video she made. Some families use standardized testing once a year in addition to a portfolio. How you record a child's work is up to you as long as it is within the requirements of the law.

The Early Years

For young children just learning to read and write, you may have many papers and must decide which ones to keep. The ones you decide to discard may be used to mail to relatives living far away as wrapping paper for small gifts or even wallpaper. For kinesthetic learners, you may have more photos than papers. Keep a book list of most of the books you read, or if you borrow books from a library, ask for a list of the books you have checked out. I used to print this list from our library at the end of the summer and highlight which books each child read in a different color. In addition, it may be helpful to take photos of the book covers as a record of what was read. Be creative in how you record books, magazines, movies, and television shows, but be thorough in recording them. Starting the first day of homeschooling, you might just stuff papers in a box. If this is the least you do, you will have something to look back on and measure progress, see what the child studied, and have a place to start next time. Take the best artwork, writing, or math papers, and put them on the refrigerator. Then at the end of the month, put them away in a box.

Keep some of your child's papers. This is nice to have to look back on and compare their progress from year to year. Keeping a few papers, drawings, files, or photos of what the kids have done helps you prepare for the next year. In the younger years, I found it easier to keep a weekly log of what we did because it was not always planned. I had a notebook with "Fragmentary Account" written on the top line and days of the month down the left side. When I remembered, I wrote a one-line account of what each child did that day. I found many more educational opportunities just happened while living our lives than what we had planned to do. At first, it was frustrating to me to keep getting offtrack and have life interrupt our educational plan. Then I began to accept the interruptions and see them as opportunities to gain experience and to show our children how to cope with disruptions in life. At the end of the school year, I compared this list with the goals I had set out to accomplish and matched up the subjects. You may start to see how several different disciplines are mastered through one experience. A day taking Grandma to the doctors can be a lesson in science, history, and poetry. Write it down, or have your child communicate what she did. Later, you will see how many different "school subjects" are learned when you least expect it.

Some families enjoy creating elaborate photo albums. One family I know created a book of their homeschooling adventure each year and even had it published for their kids to keep. What a memoir to have!

The Middle Years

Middle school can be a busy time with a lot of activities, books, and papers. This is a good stage of development to teach your child to start keeping records of his or her own learning and progress. As you start to understand her learning style, incorporate record keeping into the routine. One year, our daughter made her own portfolio, which was like a yearbook of her accomplishments, including printed photos of her doing the activities she most enjoyed. Many people don't realize you can include movie tickets, bus passes, museum pamphlets, and other ephemera in your records. Older children can help younger ones create an artistic portfolio. Take photos of places, people, and events as well as samples of writing, art, and math work, and then create a slide show or photo album for documentation and to share with family.

Below is a simple but profound poem our daughter wrote.

There was an old birch tree ...

With its old peeling bark ...

And there sat a tiny little bird ...

Every day ...

Every winter ... (E. Claus, age ten)

High School

Starting at age thirteen, when a child can complete high school level work, she can begin to earn high school credit. If you are keeping your own records, start right away by making a list of courses and resources, including books, the teacher's name, a brief description, and course dates.

Include anything related to the subject, even if it was only for a brief time. I also included how the course was taken, whether independently, online, or with a group. You can add together all the descriptions, different resources, and time periods later to equal partial or full credit for a course. I wrote course descriptions on index cards, and later when I was creating a transcript, I put those descriptions together to equal credits. When my kids went to Worldview Academy, a weeklong, intense camp that included over twenty-five hours of lectures on worldviews and apologetics, I wrote notes about it on an index card. Between that and the reading they did to prepare for their time there, they earned half a credit in apologetics for high school.

There are so many resources available to homeschoolers. Be inquisitive, and look around. You will begin to see opportunities you never imagined. As you pray for your children, look for those new and diverse ways of learning that include your passions and those of your children.

CHAPTER 7

Creating the High School Transcript

EJC photography

High school educational records should be more formally documented than those in lower grades. You might think you know whether your child will attend college or not after high school, but many times their plans change. They meet new people, find a passion for which they decide they need more education, have opportunities arise for employment or travel, or are awarded a great scholarship to attend college and decide to try it. If you don't want to write your child's transcript yourself, you can pay for a service to keep track of the courses your child took and to write one for him. This is available online and through private schools. You need to sign up for it before the school year begins so they can start keeping records through your monthly reports. Find a way to record what your high school student accomplished.

How Much Content Equals One Credit?

Depending on the materials used, three quarters to one full textbook is equal to one high school credit. High school level work is credited by a high school level textbook, online program, or in-person class that is designed for high school or college level. There are times when students don't complete the book or they supplement the textbook with more materials. As a result, they may not finish the textbook by the end of the school year. Although it varies from state to state, a homeschool's schedule may not have to coincide with any other school. Our homeschool year started September 1 each fall because we decided to start then, and it legally ended one year later, August 31. We took breaks, vacations, and snow days when we wanted to. With homeschooling, the student often has the choice of continuing to finish the course or end it and move on.

As the principal, guidance counselor, and parent, you set the learning pace, and you know your child best. Be honest with how well she scored when giving grades, not only based on tests but also on proficiency in materials, dedication to the studies, enthusiasm about the subject, and ability to communicate what was learned. Allow flexibility in how you figure out the grades so that you can give credit with consideration of all learning styles. Many standard tests are designed for only one learning style. You can create a rubric that considers multiple learning styles and include an assessment of her mastery based on her primary learning style.

How Many Hours Equal One Credit?

Some people count credit hours. The problem with this is that children each learn at a different rate. Once you get to know your child's ability to learn a topic, you will see how fast he makes progress and studies a subject to satisfactory understanding. This may also change with maturity and depend on how interested he is in the subject. As a general guide, 150 hours of study on one subject is equal to a high school credit. For some students, it takes more time, and for others, less time. Look at your goals for comprehension, test for knowledge and understanding, and then award credit hours honestly.

How Do I Write Course Descriptions?

Course descriptions are easy to write when you are using a course online, from a DVD, or from a college or university because you can obtain the information from the source. If the student is using a textbook, include a description from the inside of the book, back cover, or table of contents. When you are creating the course yourself, writing descriptions can be a little more challenging. After deciding on materials and writing an outline, I made a brief list of goals I wanted the kids to accomplish. After the course was finished, I reassessed the goals and wrote a course description based on what was done. Since I was the teacher and creator of the course, I was able to tailor it to each student's learning style. I designed many classes myself because I really enjoyed planning and creating the content and learning with the kids. Choosing and obtaining books at thrift stores, yard sales, and homeschool book sales was a hobby of mine. We also went to the local library weekly to find books we wanted to read relative to the subjects we were studying.

For example, in our study of wildlife ecology, I put together a book list, offered group classes on tree identification and wild edible plants of New Hampshire, and took the kids through fields and forests as labs. To test their knowledge, I had them pick and eat berries and leaves from the yard (with supervision), hunt and cook wild mushrooms, and introduce their friends to different species of toads and salamanders. In day-to-day conversations, I heard them discussing the ecology of the forest, evidence they saw of the history of the land, and how it was once used. Course descriptions are needed for college applications, but keeping these records early in your child's high school career will be helpful, even if she doesn't pursue higher education.

Here is an example of a course description for wildlife ecology:

> Wildlife ecology with labs: Study of the natural world is explored in detail in this course. Students learn to identify plants and animals and their habitats in their own backyard. Labs include field trips in the forests of their region to find native flora and fauna, changes in forest life over time and seasons, and care of native species in an enclosed ecosystem. Teacher: Mrs. Claus. Resources: *The Nature Book* by A. W. Thor and *The Forested Landscape* by W. R. Tirr.

What Can I Include for High School Credits?

There will probably be times when you feel like no one is "doing school" due to family illness, a job, travel, moving, or other circumstances that come your way. This is a wonderful time to keep notes or a slide show showing what your family did each day. Perhaps you all spent a few months helping a grandparent recover from an illness. If you think about it, you will see many things that the kids learned during that time. A few I think of in that situation might be geography while traveling, elder care as they learn what special aids are needed to maneuver a wheelchair around, and health as they learn to prepare a specific diet. Children also might spend many hours reading independently. Record what they read, and ask them what they learned. Perhaps Grandma will teach a child how to crochet while she's recovering from surgery. That's arts and crafts! They can bond and hear stories of her childhood, learning history. While the disruption of your regular routine may appear to be an unsurmountable mountain, take it as a life lesson to learn how to navigate challenges that arise. Life is full of surprises and opportunities.

How Does a High School Student Earn College Credits?

Earning college credits in high school is quite common. Students can earn college credit and even an associate degree while in high school. For homeschoolers, the college level course counts for both high school and college credit. For example, our son earned an associate degree in liberal arts his junior and senior years of high school. While he earned only one high school credit for each course, he earned three college credits for each. By the time he finished high school, he had earned sixty-two college credits at an incredibly discounted rate of only $100 per course. We were able to schedule his ceremonies so he graduated from the university a week before graduating from high school! High school students can take courses online or take them in a local college or university on campus. You may be surprised to find that the college-level courses are not much different from a high school course, especially if your student is already taking advanced courses or honors classes in high school.

Where Does a High School Student Get a Diploma?

Homeschoolers can buy a diploma—a piece of paper telling where and when they graduated high school. Or if part of an organization, they can be awarded a diploma. We found a template online and printed our own diploma. It is the high school transcript that is the legal documentation for graduation, not the diploma.

If you and your child decide they want to complete high school in a private or public school to earn a diploma from an accredited school, check with the school in advance and find out what they require for prerequisites so the student can prepare. In our experience, after sophomore year, it gets harder for a homeschool student to get accepted into a public high school. Schools want to see proof that the student meets their standards. It isn't always easy to adjust to the new standards and patterns of a formal school, so give your child time to prepare and adapt. Keep open communication with your child, and allow her to express how she feels and what is going on in the new situation. This is also wise whenever you move or have life circumstances that cause substantial changes for your family. Taking time to listen to your older children gives them a sense of security and connection. This is when you'll have a great impact on how your child prepares for adulthood. You have an opportunity to surround them with love and be a godly example as they navigate this journey of life.

What about Graduation?

Yes, homeschoolers do have graduation ceremonies, wear a cap and gown, and have parties if they want to. It all depends on how connected they are with other homeschoolers and how motivated they are to arrange the ceremony. The homeschool families we knew held a graduation at a local summer camp every year. Some years there were three students and other years there were ten, but the whole community of homeschoolers showed up in support. The graduates had caps and gowns, were awarded certificates or diplomas by their parents, and had a party afterward. Many home educators plan a local group graduation ceremony. In addition, students who earn a degree through a university or college can participate in that school's graduation ceremony.

What Records Are Needed for College Admission?

Colleges want to know what your child will contribute to their school, so show a good transcript, but also list volunteer work, jobs, sports, and if your child has run a business or been employed. Think of the transcript as a resume. It should show what the student has done as well as what he or she offers the institution they are applying to. This is when you will need all those course descriptions you wrote. All through the college admissions process, I had the course descriptions ready. I had worked hard to write each one carefully with dates the course was taken, who the teacher was, books or DVDs used, and a brief description of what was mastered. At first, I thought it was all in vain. It wasn't until the very end of the college admissions process that the university asked for the course descriptions. I was thrilled that I had it ready when it was needed!

Add an explanation if, for any reason, your child does not have a stellar transcript. Many homeschoolers earn far more credits than the average twenty-four high school credits required. Circumstances, such as moving during high school, family illness, or a national pandemic, can limit what they are able to do. If your student is usually dedicated and hardworking but her transcript doesn't show that, look for an opportunity to explain why or to prove that she is. Don't make excuses for laziness, however.

Ask for an in-person interview with an admissions counselor or head of the department of the college she is looking at attending, if your child is better at speaking than writing. We wanted to speak with the admissions representative and meet the professors before our children applied to a college or university. We visited one college twice, first to see the campus and a second time to meet the staff. When our son spoke with the head of the art department, he knew at once that the program was not going to be a good fit for him. As the consumer, do your research and connect with the faculty, not only buildings and grounds, when seeking a college or university to attend. Meet the staff in the department your student is considering and, if possible, the professors your child will be learning from. By talking to current students in the halls or cafeteria, you may hear a less biased opinion than those who give the admissions tour and are paid to promote the school.

If your child doesn't meet all the requirements of admission, call and ask if it is worth applying anyway, if that is what the student wants. Don't give up! Our son found colleges that did not require SAT scores because he did not want to take the SAT tests. Although the school he wanted to go to advertised that they required it, when he called and asked, he found out that they had just waived that condition for admission.

If your child has a basic transcript, they can take a college course or two to prove themselves. A semester or two of good grades from part-time college classes shows effort to succeed. Be persistent. Remember you are the consumer.

So whether your state requires you to keep records or not, you should develop a way to document what your child studies. You'll be thankful you did when you come to the high school years and are making decisions about curriculum, school attendance, post-high school plans, and writing a transcript. Prepare your student to keep records of what she studies, including hobbies, leisure reading, and activities she is involved in. These are all part of her lifestyle of learning and help to shape and develop her background knowledge. Don't dismiss the countless hours she spends getting just the right camera angle, the 5,000 photos of cats stored on an external hard drive, or the collection of vintage cameras getting dusty on the shelf. These all add up to more than just a passion or content for a course description. They show her love for learning and are an expression of her personality.

CHAPTER 8 ·

Challenging Common Myths

EJC photography

Challenge common myths, and don't get caught up in negative stereotypes associated with homeschooling. It is up to you to challenge what they're saying. History is made by people who stand out from the crowd, do the impossible task, and challenge injustice. I dare you to give your children a greater education, to foster an environment that promotes independent thinking, and to break the social agenda that the public school system promotes as healthy and normal.

This chapter will address several myths about homeschooling and why they are wrong.

Homeschoolers Don't Get Socialized

To start with, you need to define the word *socialization*. Many people think that standing in line, waiting your turn, raising your hand to ask a question, and sitting quietly at a desk for hours at a time are important social behaviors that homeschoolers miss out on. Ask curious friends and relatives what they mean by *socialized*.

I personally didn't learn my best social behaviors at school. I learned them at home from my parents and my friends' parents, older siblings, and the people in my neighborhood and by interacting in my community in an organic environment. When I went to the hardware store with my dad, I witnessed how he held the door open for people, shook hands with the neighbor we saw there, and complimented the clerk at the store for helping him find what he needed. In school, surrounded by a throng of students all within six months of my age, I learned to tease and to make fun of others, to cut in line to be next to my friend, and how to sneak notes across the desks during class.

A school classroom is often grouped by social cliques: the jocks, the geeks, the snobs, etc. The structure of the curriculum is such that students are forced to learn the same material at the same speed. This is likely the only time in a person's life when they are corralled together with others of the similar age, demographic, and culture. There is little age difference among most public school students; thus, they create a social uniformity. But in a homeschool group setting, there can be students of many ages working alongside each other and with a variety of teachers from the community.

My husband shares his experience.

> In grade school, I was learning to interact with only people of the same demographic and age. I learned to survive on the playground by adopting the gang mentality of those who pick on weak and different kids. I learned to bully the smaller, younger children. Another social lesson was boy/girl interaction without supervision or guidance. Middle school kids used foul language towards one another. The ratio of student to adult was 25:1. I was often bored because I finished my work early and had to wait for all the other students to finish or listen to the teacher explain it repeatedly.

Which is better: kids in a haphazard monoculture with minimal adult supervision learning social behaviors from each other or kids in real-life social settings under the guidance of loving parents who are intentional and purposeful about their child's development and invested in their well-being?

Homeschoolers often work with people in the community. Just as students in public or private schools, homeschoolers also work in groups and on teams, sharing project responsibilities with other students of similar age, in classes, in cooperative groups, or when taking part in a class at a local school or online program. They learn to communicate with others who have varying experiences, viewpoints, and opinions.

Homeschooling families bring together their resources and knowledge to share educational presentations. Once a year, we held International Night, a night when families each gave a presentation about a different country of the world. The displays were elaborate and involved food and authentic clothing. Students were given a passport to stamp as they traveled from country to country tasting cuisine and learning from the other families. Parents with different talents and skills offered classes on everything from art to zoology for either just a few students or a larger group of twenty kids. Moms met regularly to share curricula and ideas and to plan activities. Dads organized a BattleBots competition whereby families built remote-controlled vehicles or devices to compete in challenges, such as hill climbing, sumo wrestling, and demolition derby.

In addition to parents hosting social events, students arranged their own groups based on their interests. Students organized their own chess club, book clubs, boffer battles, hikes, and soccer games. And homeschool families I interacted with hosted weekly playground days and beach days and organized ski and ice-skating clubs in the winter. In addition, we held a monthly game night, with up to thirty-six kids attending, with outdoor games like Frisbee and capture the flag, and ping-pong and board games inside.

Although different from a traditional school setting, homeschooling creates many opportunities for rich social interaction. (Homeschool graduate)

Everywhere you go is an opportunity to learn. There are people to meet, new adventures to behold, and things to explore. Each person is unique, has a story to tell, and has information that can help you learn something new. We got to know the store clerks and postal workers on our daily trips. We learned that Julie, the sweet older lady who worked at the pharmacy, was also a teacher at a private school and lived up the road from us. Len and Lucy, who lived right next to us, volunteered at the fire station. The auto mechanic downtown, where we took our vehicles for repairs, also lived up the street from us. We took our lawn mowers to his garage when they needed to be fixed. When we asked these people about their jobs, we learned many were willing to share their passions or hobbies. For example, our neighbors the Bennett family liked to ride snowmobiles and had almost seven hundred acres of forest with well-maintained trails. After striking up a conversation, they let us walk the trails all summer and ride our four-wheelers, snowshoe and ski on their trails, and sled down a big hill in winter. They even gave us a map of their area. We used these miles of trails to forage for wild edibles, locate fresh water, and practice compass navigation when the kids were studying the Lewis and Clark Expedition. Explore your local community, and see whom you meet and what educational adventures you experience.

As part of our homeschool portfolio, we took photos and saved business cards and brochures of the places we visited. We found running errands much more interesting when we made them an adventurous field trip. I was often surprised by whom we met and where we were invited to visit. Whether it was an invitation to see a garden, special breed of cat, miniature horse, or antique car or to have tea with a couple from Germany, we met unique people with special interests and talents and learned something new.

If you explain that you are a homeschooler, you can often get a free tour of a local business or municipal building. I find that people are usually more than willing to tell what they know about a subject to curious, well-behaved children. At a local manufacturer, my kids asked questions and soon were invited to have a tour of the facility and learn how the systems worked and what the employees' jobs were like. We were given tours of stores, the town hall, restaurants, and historical buildings. People in town were willing to share their stories when they heard we were homeschooling and then offered more connections for us, introducing us to more people or setting up meetings for us. As you can see, our homeschooling experiences included numerous opportunities for rich social interactions.

I have met just as many kids who are shy and awkward in social situations who attended public school as I have in the homeschool community. (M. J. Claus)

When I was young, I was one of the most socially awkward, people-phobic kids ever. I had extreme anxiety about returning to school every fall, even when I knew all the teachers and most of the kids. For most of sixth grade, my dad drove me to school each morning because I would cry just thinking about being stuck on a bus with all the other kids for an hour to school and home again in the afternoon. It was only a twenty-minute drive without the stops to pick up other children. I was put in a special counseling group to help me adjust socially and express my feelings.

Another cause of my social anxiety was that I was forced to stand in front of the class every week and recite a poem from memory. They started out short in the beginning of the year but increased in length and complexity, and so did my anxiety. Being forced to stand in front of the class did not help me overcome anxiety. I wasted so much time worrying about reciting the poems that I didn't remember anything else I learned that year. Forcing me to do what was so unnerving detracted from my education. Part of me wishes I had had the opportunity to be homeschooled that year; I could have learned about current events, history, and so much more from my dad, a WWII veteran.

I attended public school my whole life. Being socially awkward isn't a symptom of being home educated. It is a personality trait and behavior. In this society, where there is so much emphasis on diversity, why do we make kids sit at desks facing forward and raise their hands to ask questions? There are introverts and extroverts in public schools and in the homeschool community.

I find it interesting that so many people stereotype homeschoolers as needing socialization when the public school grade and class system primarily limits students' social interactions to those of a similar age and demographic. Often, homeschooled children are funneled into that stereotype, but other educational systems funnel kids into a structure that only exists during schooling years and not in actual family, work, or social life. See how creative and socially competent your children can be when you are no longer trying to make them stand in line, sit still, or select from a list of predetermined answers in a multiple-choice format.

Homeschoolers Don't Get to Have a Graduation

Do homeschoolers graduate? This question is often followed by a sad look and comment about homeschoolers missing out on having a prom. These seem to be popularly recognized milestones for public school supporters and private schools as well. I'd say it really depends on the family and what connections they have as to whether they participate in a graduation ceremony or not. Our group of homeschoolers arranged their own graduation ceremony at a local summer camp for many years. Even though the group was small, they bought caps, gowns, and tassels. The students arranged the ceremony, hired a photographer, invited a speaker, and had a reception afterward. Friends and relatives joined the celebration and watched the students cross the stage as their parents awarded them a diploma or certificate of completion. Although not all homeschoolers have a group graduation, many do. The homeschool families get to customize the whole ceremony and make it into a small, or large, celebration to fit their unique style.

As for proms, this is also an individual decision. In the rural area where we live, our kids had a choice of three homeschool proms to attend. The most popular one had seventy kids attend the year our son graduated. They also had formal and semiformal dances, the most popular being a masquerade ball for which the attendees arrived in costume. There was no lack of celebration or attendees at these parties. One year, our son attended three homeschool proms. Yes, homeschoolers do go to the prom!

Parents Need a Degree in Education to Homeschool Their Children

Many people think that they need a background or degree in education to instruct their own children. While it is true that certified teachers have specialized education and experience in teaching methods, it doesn't mean that parents without a degree can't teach their children well. You don't get a certificate to become a parent, and you don't need a certificate to provide a good education for your child. There are many resources available for parents to use if they need help teaching a subject they are not familiar with or if their children have difficulty learning. Homeschool support groups are a great resource to find help. In some states, homeschoolers can get learning assessments and seek help at the local public school. Private schools offer classes for homeschoolers that might help when a parent desires to have someone else teach courses, such as reading, English, or math. Community services aren't free, but professionals can be hired to assess learning difficulties or behavioral issues that need to be addressed. Seek help for these learning challenges before a child is past school age.

Homeschoolers Aren't Prepared for College

Some people say that homeschoolers aren't prepared for college and don't get accepted into college. That is not our experience at all. Those who want to pursue higher education certainly can. Homeschoolers have opportunities to take college classes early too. Starting at age sixteen, high school students can take college courses for a reduced rate. There are sometimes prerequisites, but if the homeschool student meets these requirements, they are eligible to apply. You and your child should really consider what he or she needs to learn for what they want to do before entering college.

Many homeschoolers become self-motivated, independent learners (that's our goal!), which can make learning in a traditional college setting tedious, monotonous, and boring. Our son found that the online college courses he took while in high school were all formatted identically, just with different course material plugged in. He was expected to read, watch lectures, write a multipage summary, and answer questions in a discussion forum, whether it was a course in art, science, literature, etc.

This is not the experience for every student. Other homeschoolers we know went on to college and enjoyed the experiences. Our son went on to a traditional university and loved meeting in person for his first semester. In the spring of 2020, when all in-person classes came to a halt, the quality of the instruction and the value of the content diminished. This was the case for the remote learning, and it bled into the in-person courses as well when they resumed. He returned home to teach himself what he wanted to know about computer programming and graphic design, following our examples, and starting his own business.

Our daughter decided to finish high school early because she wanted to move on to do other things. She wanted to travel, visit her grandparents, and start working after high school. For now, she isn't interested in college but knows it is an option if she decides she needs training or certification in a certain area.

Your Challenge

So many myths about homeschooling are circulating. Don't let them stop you from exploring it as option. Challenge these myths. In many states, your homeschooled students can join in sports, clubs, and standardized tests at the local school and pursue a job or internship, but they don't have to in order to get "socialized." Surprisingly, homeschoolers do get bullied, have fights with others, and experience peer pressure. Though difficult, it is not always negative to experience these things. Dealing with these situations is the way in which they learn to overcome adversity. More often in a homeschool setting, parents are at the ready to help a child through these challenges—observing, counseling, and intervening if necessary. Speak up, be bold, and be creative. Bust these myths about homeschooling circulating in your sphere of influence.

CHAPTER 9

Cultivating a Lifestyle of Learning

EJC photography

Learn Something New

"What did you learn today?" was the question my dad asked me every day after school. We do indeed learn *something* new every day. For my husband and me, one of our goals for homeschooling was to cultivate a lifestyle of learning. We gave our children enough free time to explore their interests and provided them with materials and resources to do so when we could. Activities that spark joy in us help us to remember information or facts about any subject. In other words, to learn! Find ways to make learning fun, allowing children to explore their interests, and this will give them a positive experience surrounding learning. Our adult children continue to study what they want to know, following their interests, even though they are not in school anymore.

I found that allowing my kids to explore their interests gave them the freedom to follow their passions. They learned faster and more thoroughly when they could choose what to study. I called this delight-directed learning. Learning requires skills and tools. They focused on the topic of interest, not the task or the toolbox. I was there to help them acquiring the skills—brainstorming, researching, collaborating, planning—and the tools—math, reading, writing, sketching—they found were needed to pursue their interests. Then I would ask for a list of resources, such as books, magazines, online tutorials, and science or art materials, without seeming too interested, because if they thought I was telling them what to study, they might resist. I kept the list of resources so that I could write a good course description for a portfolio or high school transcript. Recording a very brief description of what they studied on sticky notes, I later assembled like subjects together. Their interests varied from science and nature to geography and writing.

Delight-directed learning, also called self-directed learning, was perhaps the most inspirational way my children learned. The topics they decided to learn were not always the ones I would have chosen for them, and more than ten years later, they still explore, enjoy, and educate themselves on activities of their own interest. Our son started computer programming when he was eight, and he has since taught himself many computer programming languages and has incorporated them into his professional development. Our daughter started using a camera at an early age, completed several online photography classes, and now does freelance photography. See examples of some of her photos in this book!

Make Time for Learning without Boundaries

Don't set time limits unless you must. Let your child spend as much time as she wants on a subject if she is gaining knowledge. For example, does your son spend countless hours playing with LEGO bricks? He can learn history, mechanics, technology, manufacturing, marketing, plastics, character development, popular movies, and literature. The popular building blocks companies follow the media industry and come out with sets of the characters. If you take it a step further, have your child research the marketing strategies and watch the movie that the toys were created for. Through local competitions or a robotics club, your building enthusiast can have plenty of social interaction and gain team-building skills. My son said, "I was curious. I wanted to learn." He explained that through his many hours of block building, he learned mechanics and physics. He explored robotics and power functions by using motors and remotes. He most enjoyed creating things that move to carry out a task in his homeschool LEGO BattleBots Club. He built a BattleBot that had everything it would need to complete a task, such as a grabber, pusher, arms, etc. He spent a year making a gyroscopic sphere, and even though it never worked as he intended, he learned a multitude of useful scientific lessons.

After our son and his best friend read LEGO Bionicle stories, they were inspired to create their own tale and characters. They spent over five years making a three-foot tall character with all mechanical moving parts until one left for college and the other friend joined the air national guard. Over the years, our son explored many careers based on his passion for LEGO bricks, including engineering and manufacturing, although he eventually pursued a degree in digital arts and graphic design. His specialty is pixel art, which is a method of creating a picture out of tiny, colored squares. What he practiced his whole life in a tactile manner, he now enjoys doing digitally. It took me years to understand that what he was doing as a kid was developing his talents for a path of study and career someday. The time he had to explore, design, engineer, and build functional objects helped him develop skills he uses in adulthood as a pixel artist. He understands how characters move and how objects relate to one another. His artistic designs are created from square pixels much like the plastic bricks and parts that he played with fit together. When he wants to learn how to do something, he studies and then practices it until he accomplishes his goal.

Passion for Learning

Especially when they are young, let children discover the world around them. When you cultivate a lifestyle of learning, the skills the child needs for what they have a passion for will become important enough for the child to want to learn, even if it is difficult for them. They will be motivated to learn what they need, in order to do what they want. Our son learned to type, and his spelling greatly improved when he wanted to communicate with his friends via the internet. I had tried to teach him typing, but until he had the motivation, he resisted.

The goal of cultivating a lifestyle of learning is that children become lifelong, independent learners. Cultivate a lifestyle of learning by letting your child see you reading, researching, taking notes, and trying to understand something new. This can be a recipe, putting together a new chair, learning to fold origami, or anything else you enjoy. Your children will model what you do more than follow your instruction. As they say, "More is caught than taught."

If you give your children enough information for them to develop their own style and passion for learning, they will take the baton and run with it, continuing to study and learn for a lifetime. Let your child teach you what they just learned. Be attentive, cooperative, and understanding without correcting them or putting in your own story of how or why you would do it differently. Let them be the teacher.

Let kids discover the world around them. When you cultivate a lifestyle of learning, the skills they need will become important enough for them to make the effort to learn. Our son learned to read because he really liked a graphic novel that had just been published and he wanted to read it himself. Having it read to him wasn't as fun because he couldn't see the cartoons that went along with the story. It was a great inspiration to learn to read.

Spiral Method of Learning

The spiral method of learning is a way of revisiting concepts learned as one adds new information. The student studies a new mathematical formula and then practices formulas learned previously. It can also refer to returning to information learned in earlier lessons or in prior years when the student has gained new skills for learning and can grasp ideas at a more mature level. This worked well for us in our studies of math and history. The kids and I explored ancient times when they were very young, before they could even read. We then moved on throughout the time periods to medieval times, the Renaissance, early modern times, and modern times. By the time we reached modern times, we were studying current events, and they were mature enough to understand the news at a basic level. We then started over again in middle school with ancient times and once again in high school. This allowed them to weave new information with old and express what they learned in new ways as they progressed in their understanding and their ability to communicate. The spiral method can be used in any subject. You may find that some curricula doesn't use this method. You can then take earlier lessons and quiz your children to find out what they remember. Look for the spiral method of learning, especially in math curricula. This is a subject that needs frequent repetition as concepts build upon previous ones learned.

Finding Educational Opportunities

Make every day a learning adventure by observing what is close around you and taking the opportunity to explore and learn while you take care of your family's everyday needs. To register our vehicles, we had to go into the town hall and see the town clerk, another neighbor of ours. Just to enter the town hall was an educational field trip. It was an old, brick building with a clock tower built in 1894. With hands more than three feet long, it still strikes every hour. The classic redbrick structure stands eighty-five feet high. The front doors are architectural artwork with their ornate design and massive size. The floors are worn from over a century of townspeople traipsing in to do their legal business. Through the many years, this building has served the town in many ways. It housed an opera, police department with a jail cell in the basement, fire department with the fire whistle still in the tower, a library, and a bank. It used to be the only place for town meetings, and even the school used it for plays, productions, ceremonies, and other events. Currently, it houses the town administrative offices and other official town business offices.

We continue to hear stories of how the town hall was used at the turn of the twentieth century from people whose family had lived in town for generations. We learned what groups met there, fees for renting the dance floor, and more legends of the supposed ghost of the town hall. One errand to register a vehicle turned into many lessons about this old, historic piece of architecture and the people whom it served.

Legend has it that there is a ghost that inhabits the tower, and townspeople tell the stories of strange happenings they see. They don't know if it is a ghost, spirit, or just people making up a story for excitement. The lady who cleans the town hall, police department, and library likes to tell of the doors she finds closed, windows open, and things moved around when no one is there. Some think of it as a spirit, a demon, or a ghost, but there are so many stories about the town hall that there is no doubt it is a mystery.

When our daughter was in high school, we were invited to tour a compound of large houses. At the time, she was interested in architecture and photography. She was delighted to tour the beautiful, enormous homes with up to eight bedrooms, a library, guest quarters, and a winding staircase. Skippy, who plays darts with my husband, manages much of the estate and invited us on a tour. Since Skippy had contracted the work on the renovations projects and done some of the construction himself, he knew the unique features of the buildings. He described how the rounded staircase was built, how the ship's bar was installed in the game room, and told us of the secret doorway to the boat dock in the basement that he called the "Bat Cave." Skippy has worked for the family for over twenty-five years. He and his wife homeschooled their children, and he was thrilled to give us a personal tour of some of the houses he managed and two garages where the vintage automobiles were stored.

Multidisciplinary Learning

Don't be alarmed when your child seems to be obsessed with one topic. If you look at it carefully, you can turn it into a multidisciplinary action, incorporating all the necessary learning skills into that topic. While this seems to be easier with elementary school children, it is possible to do for any age. The older the child and the more skills they have acquired, the more you can expect of them.

Let's look at an example. For several years, we studied salamanders. There are a dozen species of native salamanders in New Hampshire. We went on many walks in search of the slippery, shy, little creatures. We carefully recorded data in our homeschool journal under topics, such as nature, ecology, mapping, and biology. My kids, in elementary school at the time, found pictures of what each salamander looked like and where to find them, thus learning research skills. We used our local fish and game department web site, learning about conservation, preservation, and wildlife management. I incorporated *Wild Times Magazine* as well as books from the library into our study. They learned the scientific names of each salamander. We studied the habitats and geographical location where we would travel, so I recorded these as ecology, wildlife, science, geography, and mapping too. One rainy day on a half-mile walk in our backyard, we counted 113 red eft salamanders. Another day, we headed out into the forest, following a snowmobile trail to a remote beaver pond to look for swampy areas where the spotted salamander makes its home. I added recreation, biology, and ecosystems to the list of disciplines. We found two spotted salamanders in a small area and recorded it as math and population density. We took a salamander home for a few months as a science lab and then let it go again. The kids had to catch food for it and keep it moist. Through the fish and game department web site, we recorded sightings of rare salamanders. The kids measured the lengths of the salamanders from tips of the noses to tips of the tails, recorded the population by noting the number we found in each area, and drafted reports, bringing math and English to the list of disciplines.

The children learned the life cycle and diet of each salamander. Using technology and visual arts skills, they created a slide show, made a video, composed and sang a song, and created a play out of salamander sock hand puppets we made. They drew pictures and made posters about the salamanders they encountered, learning graphic design and art skills. Then they told everyone about what they learned! We took guests on adventures through the forest, explaining the habitat of the red eft salamander and how to look for the red-backed salamander under logs. Asking their friends to join them gave them social skills and proved to me how much they had learned.

As you can see, one subject—salamanders of New England—turned into many lessons spread over a multitude of disciplines. The most precious outcome to me is that our kids both still love to find salamanders in our neighborhood. When we travel around the United States, our son will research what local salamanders or lizards he may be able to see. Our daughter still loves to photograph wildlife. Using this multidisciplinary approach to teaching, the kids enjoyed learning a variety of subjects, all the while following their passion for nature.

Later, when the kids were in high school, they still had time to study what they were passionate about by using a multidisciplinary approach. They had developed strong research and communication skills that were put into practice when studying a topic and then communicating what they had learned. By then, their communication styles had developed. Much to my dismay at first, our son learned to debate with everyone! Our daughter learned to demonstrate how something is done, or made, by using photographs.

Cross-Cultural Learning

I never would have thought that starting an origami class would lead to a personal visit and interview about homeschooling with two teachers from China. One day while making my plant care rounds, I saw a beautiful, green, paper tree on a shelf of an office cubicle; the tree branches were delicately folded and balanced one on top of the other. I asked Curly, the man sitting at the desk, if he had created it, and he said with a smile, "Yes, would you like it?" He also had paper roses with petals, leaves, and stems in a jar. He had created them all out of scraps of paper to decorate his desk.

He gave me the tree and said he could make another. Our friendship grew, and soon we were leading an origami class together for other coworkers and homeschool students. We took turns teaching how to fold paper into beautiful bows, boxes, and birds.

We were soon great friends, and the kids enjoyed having "Uncle Curly" over to cook dishes from his homeland China. They learned to make spicy beef and cabbage as well as shrimp and tofu while we taught him how we make our family recipe for homemade, New York-style pizza. The kids studied origami, history, culture, geography, and cooking with him and his wife. When his parents came to the United States to visit, they were extremely interested in meeting us and learning about homeschooling. They are both teachers in Xian, China. I showed them the kids' school portfolios and the history timeline our daughter had made with drawings of major events in world history. Although neither of us could speak the other's language, using pictures and hand gestures, I shared with them the way we tutored our kids. They went home, wrote about our methods, and started to incorporate delight-directed learning into their teaching despite the strict guidelines and rigorous studies they needed to present to their students. They wanted to see their students become interested in the subjects they had to teach to them.

For us, learning is a lifetime adventure, and it is perennial, occurring all year long. Some people were shocked when they heard that we didn't take a summer break. Why should we? Our kids were always learning anyway and often studied what they liked. In summer, we had to take advantage of the nice weather and abundant opportunities to visit museums and parks. Since we lived in a tourist town, there were new people visiting every weekend, and the town supplied a lot of entertainment, such as fireworks, concerts, craft shows, and ice cream shops everywhere. There were so many places to visit and new people to meet that we didn't spend much time doing the typical reading, writing, and arithmetic that took our attention in winter.

So while your goal is indeed to educate your child at home, you don't have to separate learning from life activities. Learning is a skill that is necessary for one's entire life. It takes time to understand one's own learning style. We all develop skills to learn in separate ways. Cultivate this lifestyle in *your* homeschool for your child's future.

Concluding Remarks

I hope I have explained enough about homeschooling for you to consider the cost. The homeschooling adventure is a lifestyle many families become accustomed to. Your life and circumstances are different from anyone else's, and only you can decide what you feel is best for you, your children, and their future. This may be just the time to give it a try. Often the family that tries homeschooling develops a new pathway to education that becomes a way of life. Some plan to homeschool for a season or just part of one child's school years. Bonds are formed that are unique to homeschooling families.

Prayerfully consider what is going to help you develop godly character in yourself, your spouse, and your children and what will fit your parenting styles and allow for all members of your family to succeed. Sometimes we don't realize what a great influence we have over the development of our children's habits and character. When I consider this, I am overwhelmed and feel so inadequate to be a parent, even though I have been practicing this skill for over twenty years. I humbly bow before Jesus and ask again for grace for my shortcomings, mercy for my mistakes, and forgiveness for my faults. I ask for guidance and help to serve Him in everything I do. I pray that I will speak godly wisdom or shut my mouth when I need to be silent and just listen to what my children have to say.

You aren't perfect. The education system in America has flaws. There are evil and opposition to Christian moral values everywhere we turn, but God offers hope to a hurting world through Jesus. Change starts with you.

Therefore, since we have been justified through faith, we have peace with God through our Lord Jesus Christ, through whom we have gained access by faith into this grace in which we now stand. And we boast in the hope of the glory of God. Not only so, but we also glory in our sufferings, because we know that suffering produces perseverance; perseverance, character; and character, hope. And hope does not put us to shame, because God's love has been poured out into our hearts through the Holy Spirit, who has been given to us.

You see, at just the right time, when we were still powerless, Christ died for the ungodly. Very rarely will anyone die for a righteous person, though for a good person someone might possibly dare to die. But God demonstrates his own love for us in this: While we were still sinners, Christ died for us.

Since we have now been justified by his blood, how much more shall we be saved from God's wrath through him! For if, while we were God's enemies, we were reconciled to him through the death of his Son, how much more, having been reconciled, shall we be saved through his life! Not only is this so, but we also boast in God through our Lord Jesus Christ, through whom we have now received reconciliation. (Romans 5:1–11 New International Version)

Afterword

One year ago, I was invited to join Line-It-Up Writers with published authors Patricia Hetticher, *The Forty Weeks Series* (lulu.com), and Kay Page, *Doing Time with Charlie*. These ladies have been meeting regularly for decades, sharing pieces of writing with each other, praying together, and encouraging one another. When I started meeting with them, it was during the whole pandemic panic season of 2021 and we were not allowed to meet inside the bakery where they had been meeting. We scrunched into Patti's car, all wrapped up in winter coats and scarves, eating muffins and drinking hot coffee to keep warm. Seeing that wasn't going to work for a weekly meeting place, I asked our good friend Sara Lapointe, whom I have known for more than thirty years, if we could meet at her house. She enthusiastically agreed. The format of our weekly meetings is to bring some printed writing we created and read it to the group while the others listen and take notes, and then we give each author a review. Sara makes the grammatical corrections on her printed copy.

It is with my best friend and husband, Craig, and these dedicated ladies that I have had the ability to write this book. Catherine, a homeschool graduate, helped me rearrange all the topics and taught me how to use the writing software. From her perspective as a homeschool graduate, her college education, and her training as a content writer, Catherine had valuable understanding and insight. Our children have also contributed to this endeavor in many ways. They are the subjects for many of the stories, and with their support, they helped me overcome the technical challenges I faced. *I think computers are allergic to me!*

For years, my husband and I have been talking about writing a book together. Over the years, we have learned so many things about life that we want to share with others. We wish we knew these principles when we got married, bought our own house, became parents, started homeschooling, and started our own businesses.

After seeing all that was going on in our society, media, and culture and observing the politics being injected into education, we said, "Homeschooling is going to explode. We should write a quick start guide for parents so they can hit the ground running." After several weeks of brain dumping ideas and experiences, we were able to rearrange, categorize, and associate our writings topically and structurally, distilling them into three guidelines for the processes of decision-making and action-taking. Since most people can fairly easily commit three things to memory, this was good. If you are going to remember anything from this book, remember these three concepts:

1. Know your options.
2. Consider the cost.
3. Get what you want. (Don't settle!)

These are not consecutive steps to take; rather, they frame the questions you will ask yourself as *you* gather information, develop *your* plan, and launch *your* adventure. As we look back, we have discovered that we have been using these guidelines for the last thirty-four years of doing life together.

Still, we find ourselves with more thought-provoking questions to ask readers. When you choose your curricula, co-op classes, field trips, or social gatherings, you will find yourself defining and refining your educational philosophy to guide these decisions. What values do you want to impart to your children? What are you building into your kids' lives?

What do you want their focus to be? Athletics? Recreation? Academics? Theater? Popularity? Integrity? How do you set them up for success in life?

"Why can't we all just get along?" It takes dedication, sacrifice, and collaboration to manage, operate, and run a homeschooling household. You will find a home dynamic evolve from the sharing of time, space, and commotion. You will spend a lot of time together. There is a different dimension in which homeschool families exist. How do you share spaces? Have private spaces? Set boundaries? Respect those boundaries? Get everything done? And have fun doing it?

As a child, you didn't have to make money, and now maybe you do. If your primary education has taught you to stand in line, raise your hand, and wait to be called on, then you are ready for the antiquated manner of work and obsolete method of conducting business. Or you will find that if you have developed a lifestyle of learning, then you have the foundation for success in the multifaceted, interdisciplinary, connected, kinetic, current state of getting things done and making things happen.

I truly hope this book has helped you evaluate your goals for your family and that I have encouraged you to rely on Christ, our Redeemer, in all the decisions you make. Be humble, go forth, and don't settle for less than the best you have to offer in Jesus's name.

Resources

Visit www.mjclaus.com/rescue for a free, downloadable *Action Guide,* and start your homeschooling journey today.